GERARD DEPARDIEU MY COOKBOOK

First published in 2004 by Verlag Zabert Sandmann

This edition published in 2005 by Conran Octopus Ltd
a part of Octopus Publishing Group
2–4 Heron Quays
London E14 4JP
www.conran-octopus.co.uk

ISBN 1 84091 456 4

British Library Cataloguing-in-Publication Data. A catalogue record for this book is available from
the British Library.

English language translation provided by: Translate-A-Book, Oxford, England

Artistic direction George Feigl
Photography Nicolas Bruant, Jeremy Mathur
Stylist Sandrine Giacobetti
Text Karen Howes
Recipes Laurent Audiot, Danièle de Yparraguirre
Editing Irène Barki
Production Karin Mayer, Peter Karg-Cordes
Photo-engraving inteca Media Service GmbH, Rosenheim
Printing and binding Egedsa, Spain

Photography by Nicolas Bruant / Text by Karen Howes

GERARD DEPARDIEU
MY COOKBOOK

conran
OCTOPUS

»Le repas familial gagné et offert par le père, préparé par la mère, reste le lien essentiel où se matérialisent pour l'enfant ces images du père et de la mère, sans lesquelles un être n'a pas de solidarité intérieure, et une société cesse de bâtir une civilisation. Au nom d'une science, parfois douteuse et fluctante, il ne faut pas supprimer le long et prestigieux passé d'un artisanat, qui créa nos fromages, nos vins, nos charcuteries …«

'The family meal, worked for and provided by the father and cooked by the mother, is still the essential link that plants in a child's mind those images of its parents without which an individual has no feeling of internal solidarity and a society ceases to construct a civilization. We must not, in the name of a sometimes doubtful and changing science, lose touch with the long and prestigious past of the artisans who created our cheeses, our wines and our delicatessen...'

J. Trémolière *Encyclopaedia Universalis vol. I*

CONTENTS

Introduction 10

Entrées 30

Soups and one-pot meals 62

Fish and shellfish 88

Meat and poultry 114

Vegetables and side dishes 150

Desserts 180

Index 204

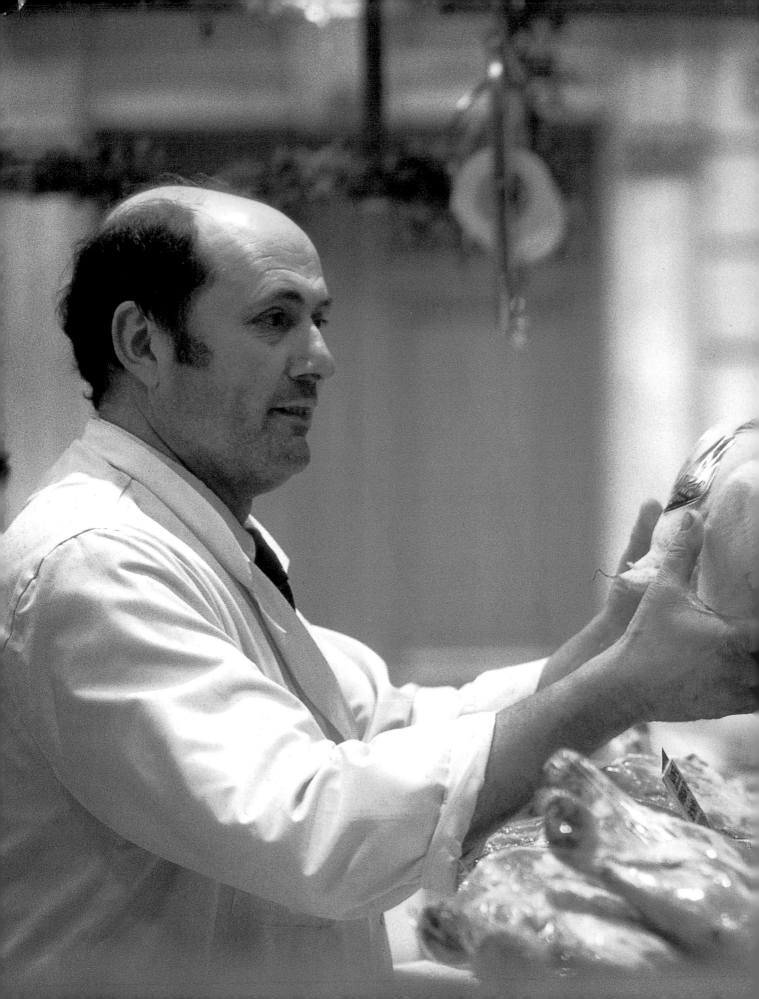

My Cooking

I have felt 'at one' with Nature all my life. I have always been alive to the variety of its smells and sounds, appreciative of its beauty and fragility and above all I have responded to its overabundance of taste and flavour. I have drawn both strength and solace from the many wonders that Nature has to offer us and to this day continue to feel at ease within its gentle embrace and in need of its daily succour.

I still feel the same intense pleasure I experienced as a child when I walk shoeless through a ploughed field after the rain – that unique sensation of wet earth squeezing through my toes and the raw smell of the soil in my nostrils. If I close my eyes, the variety of country odours distinguish themselves one from the other, the sharp tang of a confusion of wild mint, the freshness of a scattering of mushrooms in a field wet with dew, the dry, dusty quality of a hectare of ripened maize waiting to be harvested, or the scent left behind by a passing fox.

I delight in touching things with my bare hands. I prefer to eat with my fingers rather than to use a knife and fork, to feel immediately the tenderness of a cut of meat or the crispness of a vegetable. Somehow things taste different if I touch them.

I take time to look around me, to observe, not just people but also my environment, and it is not always the beautiful things in life that catch my eye, for I can be just as easily fascinated by some of its more gruesome aspects. My eye will roam with equal pleasure over the face of a beautiful woman as it will over the cuts of meat displayed in a butcher's shop window.

Of all the senses, taste is for me perhaps the most critical, whether I am trying something for the first time or I am rediscovering an old flavour. And, there

again, I have an acute sense of hearing. Sometimes it is enough just to hear part of a story for me to imagine the rest – the rustle of dry leaves in the hedgerow as a small animal scuttles back to its burrow; a bird turning over the soft earth in search of a juicy worm. Each of the senses builds a unique picture. I like to listen to the sound of a cauldron of soup bubbling gently over a low flame or the noise wine makes when you pour it from the bottle into a crystal glass. And there is especially the sound of silence. I love to listen to my own silence or to the silence of those around me, who are searching for tranquillity.

The Earth produces everything that we need to live on. Grain, vegetables, fruit and grass for the cattle, while in the forests and woods animals survive on what the trees and shrubs produce. Like all the living creatures in this world, the Earth needs water and light to survive. Everything is connected. If the Earth suffers, so too do the animals that live off the land. For, when animals graze on plants that are no longer healthy and we, in turn, eat the meat of these animals, we are creating a chain of natural disasters.

To write a cookery book is a challenge of a particular kind, for it is not just a question of introducing a selection of hitherto unknown recipes, but I want to tell the stories that lie behind the recipes as well. The ingredients are naturally very important, but so too are the people who raise the animals, who bake the bread and make the cheese, who cultivate the fruit and tend the vines. They have an inordinate pride in their profession and it has always been important for me to understand and to get to know this human element so crucial to the quality of our food production.

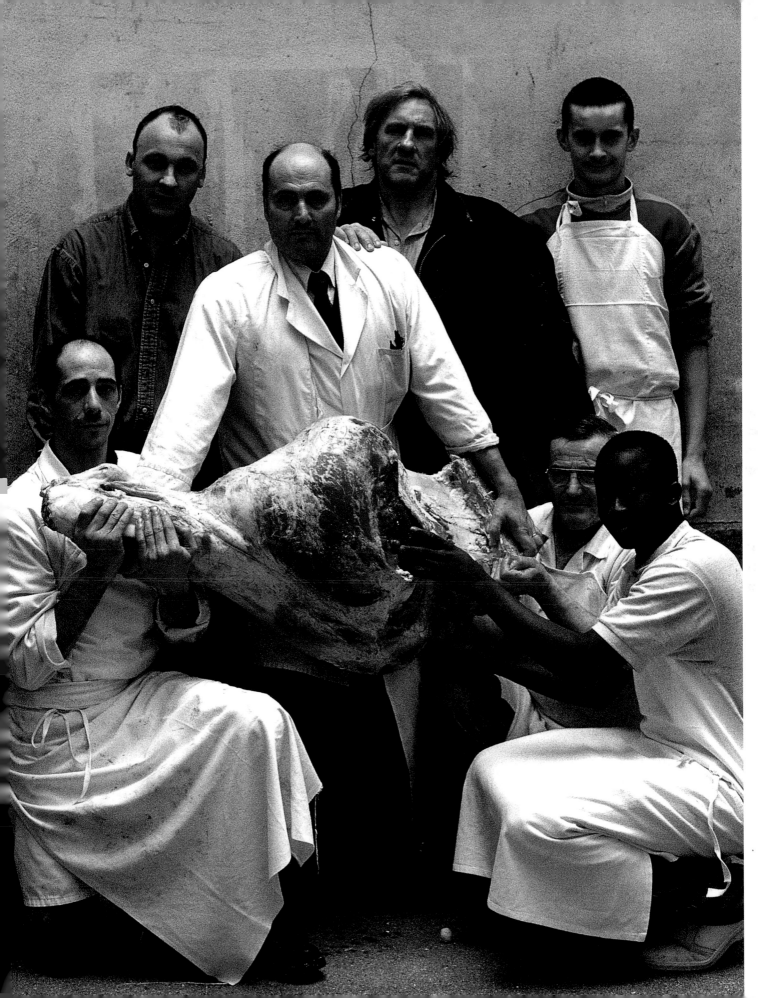

Also of importance is the person who actually does the cooking, whether at home or in a restaurant, for how that person feels – whether they are in a good or a bad mood – ultimately will affect how the meal tastes. We all know how to cook, but to cook well and for a dish to taste delicious, it must not only be made with good ingredients, but it must also be created with a positive energy, by someone who loves cooking, and who delights in the wide variety of products that are available to us today.

In my cookery book I want to illustrate that not only do we have a responsibility towards Nature, but also a duty to preserve our sense of tradition and our origins. Many rituals and customs have survived down the centuries only to fade into oblivion in the last 50 years. This is a shame, since the majority of these traditions probably served a purpose which we would do well to dwell upon. If we do not preserve our traditional farming methods for future generations, for example, our children and our grand-children will no longer know what a cow or a fish actually looks like. We need to hold onto the variety that life continues to offer us and thus keep our senses enriched. This is another reason for my book.

When I cook, I like to keep it simple. I try to make the best of each ingredient and therefore look for products that are fresh and healthy. It does not cost a great deal of money to prepare a good meal. I like simple dishes that anyone can make successfully, a combination of the traditional and the contemporary, such as *coq au vin*, *pot au feu*, *blanquette* of veal, ravioli or a freshly grilled fish.

Cooking is a totally sensual pleasure, for you must be able to smell, to touch, to taste, to watch and to listen. I remember preparing a rabbit *en gelée*, which I make frequently at my home at the Chateau de Tigné in Anjou, in the company of a great friend and fellow actor Jean Carmet. Normally, we eat it for breakfast, slathered over a slice of grilled country bread and washed down with a glass of cold white wine. It is a wonderful and recurring memory, and one of many that I hold onto. We have five senses. If we use them properly, they will help us appreciate the true simplicity behind some of life's real pleasures, such as cooking or making love, as well as the importance of sharing such rare and beautiful moments.

Cooking, like drinking a fine wine, gives me the greatest of joy, and I am at my happiest when I am preparing a meal for my family, for the children, or for my friends. For cooking is all about love, and love is strength. The art of cooking and preparing a meal to share with those you care about is also, for me, a means of communicating that love and friendship without necessarily having to utter a single word. This is also why I want to reveal in my cookery book not only how I cook and what I enjoy eating, but how it all hangs together: from the importance of mood and the best ingredients to the essential respect for Nature. I would like to be able to pass a little of this on, particularly to our children.

As a child, I was poor but free

I was born in 1948 into a large family, the third of six children. We lived in Châteauroux, a small town in the Berri in central France, which became a base for American soldiers after World War II, but which was otherwise a dull place, inward-looking and cut off from the outside world.

We were poor, but I was never jealous of those who had more than I. Instead, I would watch the people around me doing the things I could not afford to do, such as eating well or living in beautiful surroundings. I remember at the age of eight slipping out of bed one night, lured into the darkness by a travelling fairground. I was entranced by the kaleidoscope of colour, by the noise of people enjoying themselves and by the smell of sweetmeats and toffee apples. I remember it was a beautiful night, the experience of which perhaps awakened in me at so young an age the ability to imagine. In the gathering silence of that night, I remember watching the people returning home, glimpsing into the illuminated rooms of their houses, and visualizing what their lives must have been like.

I left school earlier than I would have liked, a move prompted by a misunderstanding when I was accused of a theft that I had not committed. It taught me my first hard lesson – that life does not give you everything. You have to take what you can and make the most of it. As a result, I spent a lot of time outdoors, fishing, walking and enjoying the fresh air, cultivating an appreciation for Nature and a taste for life. I call it '*le gout de la vie*', and it has stayed with me ever since. This love of life encompasses simplicity, fair play and equality. It has nothing whatsoever to do with possessions, but everything to do with the quality of life and with imagination.

When I lived at home, we would have meat for the first week of the month. If we were in credit with the butcher, we would have horse meat, which was cheaper than other meat, and in the summer sometimes a little *charcuterie*, which I loved. My father, whom we called *Dédé*, would make a stew, since dishes with lots of sauce are good for disguising potatoes and leftovers. Occasionally, *Dédé* would be lucky enough to be given a rabbit by a passing hunter, which he would prepare in a similar way. Otherwise, there were lights in gravy and always potatoes – chips or mash – as well as rice and bread, of course. When my father prepared a meal, he did it alone; I never once helped him in the kitchen. It was modest fare, but it was prepared with imagination and I lacked for nothing. To this day, meat has remained for me a symbol of prosperity.

Imagination was almost as important as the ingredients themselves. We ate like the majority of poor people, with little variety and very little meat, and tried to ring the changes with the available vegetables. In Lyon, the potato is known as the 'truffle of the poor', and it is still the most important vegetable. It is surprising how many different ways there are of cooking potatoes and leeks and, particularly with a soup, how simple it is to change the taste of the dish with the addition of just one new ingredient – a cabbage or a turnip for example. Soup was always eaten around 5 p.m. and was the traditional meal that brought the family together at the end of the day. The secret with a soup is never to add a piece of cooked meat – it must always be fresh, or you will ruin the flavour. I have always loved dishes that have been simmered for hours; they have such a strong and unique taste.

However simple, everything that we ate at home was always fresh and taken from its natural habitat, whether it was a carp caught in a neighbourhood lake, a rabbit shot in the local woods or the vegetables grown on our small plot of land. The earth in which we grew our leeks and potatoes was fertilized naturally using our own ordure, free from the sprays and pesticides that affect the taste of all the vegetables we

buy in supermarkets today. Our home-grown leeks were not necessarily any larger than normal, but they had a wonderful flavour!

The respect for food that I developed during my childhood means that I have always hated waste and try never to throw food away, preferring to turn any leftovers into another meal. The remains of a *pot au feu*, for example, can be made into a shepherd's pie, and a sauce or gravy can be mixed in with another sauce, as long as you add something fresh to it as well.

I think I have been interested in the culture behind eating and drinking for most of my life. From an imaginative introduction as a child, I became more curious as I got older, sticking my head into restaurant kitchens around the world, wherever I was filming, demanding of chefs to know exactly how they were preparing a particular dish, tasting, smelling and touching new and exciting products. I would visit the market stalls and try everything and anything that was culturally different, or meet with the artisans and share their simple meals, returning home to Paris my head filled with new ideas and recipes to try out on my friends.

And it was in a similar fashion that I discovered my passion for wine growing, by constantly tasting, smelling and questioning, although my affinity with and love of the land also had an influence. I made my first purchase over 30 years ago – 1 hectare (2.4 acres) in Bourgogne, followed in the late 1980s by the acquisition of the *domaine* of the Chateau de Tigné in Anjou, an area of 110 hectares (272 acres), which was already well established, as well as a further 2 hectares (5 acres) at Aniane in the Languedoc to produce a *vin de garage*, a wine developed following traditional methods.

I have always been keen to defend the time-honoured way of making wine, particularly in this era of mass production in which we live. To make such a wine is to know a *terroir*, the qualities of a particular soil. It is about having two or three hectares (5 or 7.4 acres) and producing the best that the soil can give you.

According to the oenologist, Jacques Puisais, 'each wine is a mirror of its environment. At one and the same time, it is the product of the earth and of the air and the child of the man who has nurtured it.' If the land is not good, there is very little you can do to improve the quality of the wine.

Wine has a soul. For me, it means being with friends and sharing the simple pleasures of life. I don't like wine to get drunk on, nor to forget. I like it because it lifts the spirit.

Contented animals make for healthy people

I have always been interested in the people who live for and have a relationship with their animals. It is quite obvious that, if the cattle on a farm are allowed to wander freely through the meadows, to feel the rain on their backs, and to experience the changes of weather and seasons, their meat will taste differently to that of cattle which are raised in wholesale fashion for mass production. I make a habit of seeking out the farmers who are proud of their animals and who consequently look after them and even accompany them to the abattoir. For these people are true artisans and their trade is the most important thing in their lives.

They understand what cows, sheep, pigs, goats, hens, geese and ducks need in order to lead a contented life. Hens must be free to scrape and peck at the earth, for they are still creatures that can fly and therefore need an open run. Pigs are curious and like to root around and also love to roll and wallow in the mud. Cows are always on the move, running hither and thither, free to roam in peace and tranquillity. They don't seem to mind the changing seasons or the fluctuating temperatures and, in fact, their powers of resistance appear to be strengthened, not weakened, in consequence. Kids and calves that are allowed to stay with their mothers grow up free of stress. Any animal that is allowed to grow up in such an environment and that receives in addition the correct natural feed is a happy animal. An animal that does not have the good fortune to grow up in this way and that, before it is slaughtered, must travel halfway around Europe, in order to meet its end in an undignified yet technically acceptable abattoir, cannot yield a meat that tastes good. It is simply impossible, and it would be better to eat no meat at all than to eat this. A quality product needs time to mature and to achieve this the responsibility is placed squarely on us and on our natural environment.

I have always believed that it is important to have not simply experts in the field of nutrition, but also people who are passionate about it, so that there is a balance between the two worlds which directly influence what we eat.

Abuse is rife in the world in which we live, because demand has outstripped our ability to supply. With the advent of the supermarkets and the massive discount stores in the 1960s and 1970s, the pressure from the consumer on the producer to supply greater and greater quantities of food has sounded the death knell for the local artisan and regional farmer.

To keep up with demand, we have resorted to chemicals to fatten our cattle artificially, our fish are injected with colouring to make them appear more appetizing and they are fed on fish meal, which goes against the dictates of everything that is natural. We have re-modelled our chickens into convenient lumps of meat that weigh 1-1.5 kg (2 lb 4 oz–3 lb 5 oz), suitable for a family of four! The industrial level to which poultry farming now aspires is conducted with such complete indifference to the wellbeing of the individual bird and in such terrible conditions, that it is hardly surprising that birds attack each other or injure themselves, when they are obliged to exist in such cramped and untenable conditions.

As the focus of attention is increasingly drawn to the plight of battery hens, a staple of our contemporary diet, and in the wake of the recent scare surrounding bird flu in Asia, as well as continuing worries over the freshness of eggs and the rise in cases of salmonella, public opinion is turning away from the mass production of meat in its various forms. A slow revolution is gathering momentum against any such chemical enhancements, such as the injection of antibiotics to ensure that an animal survives the life that we impose upon it, and other such unnatural controls over the food that we eat.

A real chicken, the *poulet de Bresse* for example, which comes from Bourg-en-Bresse, is a farm-reared chicken, which takes 16 weeks to grow (as compared with $6\frac{1}{2}$ weeks for a chicken sold through the supermarkets). Compared to its bloated commercial relation, its flesh is firm and dark in colour and it has an amazing and unique flavour. This creature will never see the interior of a battery building, for it is at liberty to scavenge for its proteins and essential nutrients from a *terroir* of marshy land. Glorified by the 19th-century French gastronome Jean-Anthelme Brillat-Savarin as 'the queen of poultry and the poultry of kings', this is the chicken that I like to eat myself. In Bresse, a chicken is often poached and served in a rich creamy sauce.

By the 1980s we began to realize that the quality of the food available to us was simply not good enough; that even the bread, still an essential part of the diet of the poor, was padded out with sugar and fat, and that the majority of meat available in the supermarkets was not what it appeared to be, but had been injected with hormones to give it more flavour. This goes against Nature. It is not normal or acceptable and is one of the principal causes of 'mad cow disease'.

In direct response to this universal demand for reassurance, the government sought to assuage our fears and introduced a system of *Appellation d'Origine Contrôlée* (known as AOC), a means of designating and controlling both the geography and the quality of a product. Specific guidelines were drawn up which producers were obliged to adhere to, and which

prohibited herbivores being fed animal hormones, for example. As the revolution against the industrialization of products and specifically the supermarkets, which we recognized as being the root cause of all this mass production, gained support, regional markets and the specialist producers began to enjoy a new popularity. As our concerns about the quality and safety of our food increased, the more we clamoured for local and regional products whose origins could be traced and relied upon.

The next development was a programme of '*Labels rouges*', or red labels, a further initiative introduced by the AOC, and a visual means of endorsing certain products as being of superior quality and, in particular, of superior flavour. For the first time we were given a guarantee that certain foods had been produced following traditional methods. Produce such as chicken, charcuterie, dairy products, seafood, fruit and vegetables, and now even certain brands of salt are all sold with a red label. The purpose of these labels is to help us distinguish between a product that

is good and one that is not, but, of course there are a number of different types of label and it has become very confusing. Not surprisingly, these 'superior' products are also more expensive and in many cases the poorer consumer is forced to continue to buy sub-standard produce.

By the end of the 1980s, as international public awareness surrounding product quality continued to grow, an association called 'Slow Food' was created in Italy by gourmet journalist Carlo Petrini. With the war cry 'eat less but eat better' the movement set out to protect our right to taste, and to encourage us all to recognize and place greater importance on regional and traditional products. They sought to protect local artisans and regional produce and to cultivate a more sophisticated palate.

Close your eyes for a moment and imagine the sensation of re-discovering the taste of an exceptional dish prepared with ingredients of an extraordinary flavour and served above all with love. This is what it is all about!

Food is also a question of culture

I have been fortunate during my career as an actor to have the opportunity of visiting many different countries and of sharing and participating in their cultures and traditions. One of the benefits of filming is that I stay in one place for several weeks at a time, which gives me a chance to look around me and to meet with the locals and to pick up on some of their cultural idiosyncrasies.

The subtleties in regional cooking in France become apparent as you travel from north to south, or east to west and each region is prized for its specialities. East, along the Loire, you have fruit, baby vegetables, asparagus and mushrooms. Follow the Charente, to the south, and you will find the best butter, and in Brittany, to the west, with the co-mingling currents of the Atlantic and the Gulf Stream, tuna, sardines, anchovy and mullet are among some of the best fish and shellfish in France. On the marshes of the Grande-Brière, you can still catch eel using

traditional methods, and lamb that is raised on the marshes is therefore 'pre-salted' from birth and is the most delicious local dish when served *à la bretonne* with dried white beans and tomato sauce.

Head southwest to Gascony and you will find pigs fed on maize and acorns gathered from the local forests. The traditional pig-killing ceremony lasts two days, during which time the intestines are cleaned for sausages, the livers are made into pâté, and there is a resultant delicious black pudding. Bayonne ham is salted for several days and then pickled in brine with red wine and herbs for at least a month, after which it is smoked in the fireplace. A coarse pepper is rubbed into the meat to ward off the flies and then the hams are hung in a cool place to age for several months. This region is also famous for its 'foie gras', whether goose or duck. In addition, the carcass is delicious roasted whole over an open fire and the white fat it produces, together with local garlic and rosemary, is wonderful for frying potatoes. The meat from a fattened goose makes the best *rillettes*, which is a type of coarse pâté baked in a sealed dish until the meat falls off the bone. Then there is *confit*, where the duck or goose is packed into a crock and sealed with fat and is cooked for a long time extremely slowly. Stored for at least a month, its flavour is extraordinary and mellow. Good food in my view is when things retain the flavour of what they are.

If we look back on our 'family' meal, the soup, it is interesting to acknowledge how many regional interpretations of this simple dish exist in France alone; from the *garbure* or vegetable soup of Gascony, which is the equivalent of Bouillabaisse in Provence, to the classic fish soup of the Languedoc known as *bourride*, a white soup served with aïoli, to mention but a few.

Yet if we are looking for significant regional differences, it is especially on the borders, where the culture of two countries overlaps, that the local cuisine is often the most imaginative.

Tradition, customs, language and religion establish the basic distinctions between countries and the resultant subtle cultural differences are reflected particularly in the eating habits of its people. While religion plays an important part in the cultural acceptability of certain food, I also believe that there is often a practical reason behind a religious edict. For example, a Muslim is prevented by his religion from eating pork. Now most Muslims live in hot climates and it is a well-known fact that pigs do not adapt easily to the heat and that pork can putrefy faster than other meats.

When I was filming *Asterix and Cleopatra* a few years ago, I was based in Ouarzazate in Morocco for several months. The Muslim culture is fascinating and I had the privilege of meeting a variety of artisans and tradesmen. I learnt about their education, their rituals, their lifestyle and their culture. I learnt how they managed to live with so little available water and that their innate sense of hospitality requires them to spare their last drop to make mint tea for their guest. In my opinion, the Muslim religion, as outlined in the Koran, is the only religion that really provides a direction for the poor.

As far as my own religious beliefs are concerned, I try to believe in God while taking into account life in general and what it has to offer us. I believe we should try to love and respect those things that surround us, not necessarily in a religious sense, but more an aesthetic one – quite simply to appreciate the beauty around us. There is a certain silence achievable when I

am at one with Nature that encourages such deep reflection that I feel I am almost in a state of grace.

In Morocco, I also learnt their way of killing an animal and of cutting up the carcass; a violent but unexpected death, and one in which the animal's throat is cut while being essentially embraced, yet a killing all the same in which the animal dies free of stress. The cultural diversity, which dictates the manner in which our animals are killed, contributes directly to the taste of the meat and it is true that a lamb killed by a Spaniard differs in flavour from a lamb killed by an Italian or by a Moroccan.

I have always believed that if an animal can be slaughtered in a stress-free way its meat tastes so much better. Before killing a pig, I will always talk to it. The pig is an intelligent animal, so much more intelligent than a dog, and it is easy to become emotionally attached. An animal that has been caressed before being killed dies peacefully and its muscles do not contract with adrenalin, for it experiences no sense of fear. I have visited abattoirs, real slaughterhouses, in the dead of night, where I have witnessed men, bored and with little else to do, torturing the animals before killing them. I can never erase those images from my mind.

Travel is the best form of education. While we think of French cuisine as being the epitome of regional cooking, it is to Italy we must turn for the simplest and the best. It does not matter where you go in Italy or into which local 'trattoria', the food is all home-made and of such a distinct quality, from their bread, desserts and cakes, to their home-made pastas and delicious sauces.

When I was filming *1900* in Italy with Bertolucci, I came across a culture which reminded me of my own. A culture of poverty shared by the Italian peasants, yet with a subtle difference. Why is it possible to eat so well in Italy? Is it simply because they still have a respect for life? The Italian cuisine has the best produce, such as olive oil and green tomatoes – you can only find such a fruit in Italy and it has such an extraordinary flavour!

Italian cooking specializes in stews and sauces and in all those dishes that take hours to cook. Dishes that simmer gently over a low heat and are made up of all the best things that come from the earth. This is my favourite form of cooking. *Bollito misto* for example, a dish of boiled meats, originated in Bologna. The Italians serve this unique dish with *mostarda*, a sweet, spicy jam full of peel, pieces of fruit and slices of cucumber. Not to be outdone, the English also eat their meat with jam, serving traditional roast leg of lamb with redcurrant jelly and mint sauce, or cold cuts with that uniquely English concoction, chutney.

Some cultural traditions can be difficult to accommodate, although I am lucky enough to have a strong stomach, in addition to a curiosity that can often get me into trouble! I remember a trip to Mauritania, for example, where I visited a baker who was so poor that he put sand in his bread. Yet, despite their obvious poverty, these people were so hospitable and they made me welcome with an offering of fresh figs served with rancid butter. On another occasion in Italy, I was offered a piece of polenta with a slice of donkey meat. Until then, I had no idea anyone ate donkey!

On another film with Bertolucci, I disappeared for a weekend into the desert with a guide and a camel. The guide had brought along a goat, which we killed that night. It was so thin, yet we cooked it with a few twigs and plants that we found in the desert and it was an extraordinary meal. From a European standpoint, I can understand that such a meal could be considered a little barbaric, yet the cultural traditions in Asia leave nothing to the imagination. In China, they eat practically anything. I believe this tradition stems from the fact that their religion is much more instinctive, and that they believe that they can become what they eat. For example, among other delicacies, they believe that eating the brains of a monkey will make them cunning and that a diet of tiger penis soup will greatly improve their sexual prowess!

What is the history behind French cooking?

Although we have a great tradition for fine cuisine in France, it was not until the Revolution that this aspect of our culture began to influence the lives of ordinary people. Until that time, the country was divided. While the peasants had to content themselves with bread and whatever they could scratch from the land, the aristocracy and the sycophants who hung around the Court were responsible for the most terrible waste of food and resources. Vast tables groaning with food would be prepared daily, with menus sometimes consisting of more than 50 different dishes. The King would pick at the selection, taste a few of them, but rarely eat more than a few mouthfuls, for at Court in those days it was just as important to appreciate the beauty of a dish as it was to actually taste it.

When I was filming *Vatel* with Roland Joffe, I played the part of a man who was the 'contrôleur général de la Bouche de Monsieur le Prince de Condé', or, put more succinctly, the man in charge of the Prince's mouth and more particularly, what he ate. In the film I have to feed 600 courtiers plus thousands of hangers-on and servants over a period of three days. It was a crime to prepare such magnificent dishes for people who could not have been less interested in food, while the real people out in the country were literally dying of hunger, with nothing but bread to sustain them. It was obvious that one day the granaries would be empty and that there would be no more wheat in the fields and that the people would eventually revolt against all this vainglorious and immoderate wastage.

The Revolution had an enormous effect on French cuisine and our whole attitude to cooking changed radically. It is from this revolution of the 'bourgeoisie' and the common man that the art of French cooking was born. The chefs who were formerly employed by the aristocracy and the landed gentry now cooked for the people. Gradually they opened restaurants, which replaced the inns and hostelries where food was never a priority, and began to teach the people how to eat well.

The beginning of the 19th century represented an important stage in the development of French cuisine and a considerable evolution in eating habits generally. Economic stability, the modernization of agricultural methods and an increase in the wealth and standing of the bourgeoisie all contributed to the boom in the restaurant business. From the fashionable restaurants of Paris to the grand country houses, the French were being encouraged to develop a more sophisticated palate, an example reinforced by the accession to the throne of France's most gourmet king, Louis XVIII.

As a result, we became obsessed with food in France and, encouraged by the new authority acquired by the chefs in Paris, we were ready to follow their lead and to move from a cuisine where dishes were more decorative than wholesome, to a stage where taste would play a leading role.

New products also became available to us. The common potato, encouraged by Napoleon, was supplemented by the introduction of rice and pasta, macaroni in particular, which was discovered while waging war in Italy. We started to grow sugar beet as a replacement for sugar cane, which was expensive, lowered prices and increased consumption and, as a result, we began to conserve our produce in cans. Other significant developments in French agriculture introduced a new choice of vegetables, such as spinach, watercress, celery and asparagus, and mushrooms started to be cultivated in Paris.

Meat, a rarity for so long, became more available. First it was poultry, a duck maybe or a goose and then beef was introduced in the first half of the 19th century, eaten as fillets with mushrooms or boiled in an onion sauce. Then came veal, calves kidneys and sweetbreads, followed by lamb and finally pork. Game, traditionally the preserve of the nobleman, also started to appear on the bourgeois menu, particularly of those who had started to acquire land and woods of their own, and gradually wild boar, hare, partridge and pigeon joined the dishes on the menu. Yet wild game is still regulated by laws which govern hunting and which date from the Revolution. Hunters may consume their own bag, but may not sell the proceeds of their kill unless it is to licensed businesses.

This meat was no longer eaten on its own but would be accompanied by rice or pasta or even potatoes, encouraging chefs for the first time to mix meat and vegetables, which had traditionally always been served separately.

As the Industrial Revolution took hold, improvements in transport enabled us to eat seafood and fish more regularly. Refrigeration was not far behind. Yet cheese was still eaten by those who could rarely afford sugar or dessert and was not considered grand enough for a nobleman's table. By the Second Empire, as with many other things, this would change.

And yet where are we today? On the one hand we have butter mountains, a superfluity of so many things which leads to extraordinary waste, and on the other we have starvation, not just in Third World countries, but at home, right on our doorstep. In the 21st century in France, as elsewhere in Europe, we still have people living below the poverty line, people who are unable to afford the good things in life. We have pollution and a continuing abuse of our animals and livestock, and thus of our nation as a whole.

I had always wanted to be a butcher, but in the meantime I became an actor, and now I have opened my first restaurant. Following almost 20 years of thinking about it, I met Laurent Audiot who was working in a wonderful fish restaurant in Paris called Marius et Janette, just around the corner from my office. Laurent is a great chef and we share the same passion for food and for wine. I promised him that we would work together one day and here we are. The chef is an important person, the integral soul of a restaurant, even a confidant. Perhaps in this new role of restaurateur I also see myself as being able to influence, if only in a small way, how we can all learn to appreciate once more the essence of good food and great wine.

La Fontaine Gaillon, my first restaurant, is a logical progression of my diversification into the wine industry. But, as with everything, I am unable to stop there. I will soon be opening a bistro across the square from the restaurant where you can try all sorts of different wines, learn of their provenance, distribution, etc. and eat a small something while you are at it. And then I have opened a bakery, and this will soon be joined by a grocery store… And then there are several other projects on the boil – maybe a couple more restaurants like Fontaine Gaillon in other countries.

As Balzac put it so beautifully, 'the trouble with life is not its duration, but the quality, the variety and the number of sensations we need to experience.'

We have a legacy to leave to our children

Nature has everything to offer us and, in turn, we must understand Nature in order to cook well and to produce good wine. Nature is powerful, determined, positive, multifarious, gentle and dangerous, all at the same time. We will never be able to tame it or to make it work to our advantage, but in understanding its depths, the riches and the variety it has to offer, we can surely learn to appreciate Nature and to live in harmony with it.

What we learn from the produce on sale in the markets is that we cannot change the order of the seasons or the rhythm of time. We should always eat those things that are fresh and in season, to savour the moment when the first sweet strawberry heralds the arrival of summer, or when the scent of roasting chestnuts announces the onslaught of winter. I love to eat fruit when it is in season. The taste of a cherry

ripened by the sun and eaten at the height of summer bears no comparison to a cherry that has been kept in cold storage and brought out in deepest winter. I hate eating cherries at Christmas!

Yet it is difficult to change the habits so ingrained in our culture today. It is true that a good quality of life has become more affordable, but the one thing we do not have enough of is time. Today, the majority of mothers and women work, and they have less time to look after their children. Obliged to shop in their lunch hours or to make a quick stop at the convenient local supermarket on the way to picking up a child from school, it is simpler to opt for a pre-prepared frozen meal than to buy fresh produce in the market.

If we lived our lives differently, we should throw out our microwaves and re-discover the dishes that our grandmothers used to make; recipes in which the taste of the meat is redolent of the charcoal on which it is grilled, and where the preparation of a meal can take anything up to five hours. Roast knuckle of milk-fed veal with vinegar (see page 120) and Pork loin stuffed with herbs (see page 136) are just two examples.

An added problem is that our children no longer want to eat things that they recognize, like the chickens which they see running around on television, or the fish in the local aquarium. What they prefer is fish that looks like two fingers or a square nugget. Our children will always be followers of fashion. My daughter, Roxanne, for example, is at the 'hamburger stage', but she is starting to eat more real meat and gradually I will introduce her to new dishes and show her what is essentially good to eat.

We have a duty to our children to educate their taste in food and not to allow them to be influenced entirely by the inevitable success of the 'fast food' chains. It is important to listen to a child's likes and dislikes and to steer them slowly but surely away from the food which is high in sugar and fat but which, for just that reason, inevitably tastes so much better in their eyes.

I have never forced a child to eat against their will. There is too much injustice in the world to force food down the throat of an unwilling infant, but if you show an enthusiasm yourself, this will encourage the child to try something new and to begin to understand the different flavours and the variety that is Nature's gift to us.

So much is down to basic education. I remember a day when the daughter of American actress Jamie Lee Curtis came with her mother to visit. There was a cherry tree in the garden and the little girl did not know what it was. She did not understand that a cherry tree produced cherries. Understandably, she believed that cherries grew in a punnet. Even Peter Weir, the Australian film director, was astonished to see the variety of vegetables growing in abundance in my kitchen garden, when I asked him what he wanted to eat for lunch. In particular, he could not believe the endives growing in the dark of my cellar! Yet, it is not necessarily down to ignorance that we do not know these things; it is more a question of culture.

A little knowledge can also be dangerous. As we have slowly come to understand certain things about our diet, what is good for us and what is bad, we have fallen victim to a new craze. In America, for example, the emphasis now is on 'low fat' and the concern is about fat and cholesterol. So we now buy our food with a view to losing weight, despite the fact that we still do not know exactly what is involved and that the manufacturers of 'low fat' products are including sugars and other carcinogenic additives in the ingredients in order to make these foods taste more interesting.

My interest in food also extends to its influence on our health and a diet every now and again is important to combat obesity. However, a diet for me begins in my head. I have to want to lose weight and with this desire I must also understand the needs of my own body. I begin by eating half of my usual daily intake and instead of bread I will eat vegetables or fromage frais, a soft white cheese. Food becomes very simple, little more than a large bowl of soup. In 10 years I have lost over 300 kg (661 lb)! Not difficult for a man who loses 30 kg (66.1 lb) a year – for I gain weight and lose it again in inevitable cycles.

Diet is again a matter of culture. According to Balzac, 'To eat and to drink require different and oft opposing qualities. Man is too imperfect to be inclined towards such noble tendencies. The man who is able to unite the qualities of a gastronome to the same degree as those of a gourmet would be a phenomenon.'

If I have an ambition still unrealized it is to tend the vines, to produce wine and to work like a true artisan. I dream of working with different soils and of re-discovering the old traditions and customs of wine growing, not necessarily to deny the technology which we have today but to harness this technology into working in harmony with Nature.

We must nurture Nature and learn to appreciate it with all of our senses.

ENTRÉES

Dishes served as entrées are light and substantial enough to be eaten at any time, even for breakfast. At home in the Chateau de Tigné, in Anjou, I often make jellied rabbit and cherish fond memories of one which my great friend and fellow actor, the late Jean Carmet, and I ate on a slice of toasted country-style bread, accompanied by a glass of cold white wine. What a marvellous way to start the day!

Marinated fresh anchovies with potatoes

PREPARATION TIME: 20 MINUTES / COOKING TIME: 20 MINUTES
STANDING TIME: 2 HOURS / MARINATING TIME: 24 HOURS / PREPARE THE DAY BEFORE

Serves 4

1 kg (2¼ lb) very fresh small anchovies · fine sea salt
For the marinade 3 garlic cloves · 2 onions · 2 small carrots
6 tbsp extra virgin olive oil · 200 ml (7 fl oz) aged wine vinegar
100 ml (3½ fl oz) water · salt and freshly ground black pepper
2 thyme sprigs · 4 parsley sprigs · 1 bay leaf
6 coriander seeds · 1 lemon
To serve 1 kg (2¼ lb) firm, waxy potatoes, such as Charlotte or Ratte

To prepare the marinade: peel the garlic and one of the onions, and roughly chop them. Peel the carrots and cut into thin round slices. Place the oil, vinegar, onion, garlic, carrots and water into a deep dish, season with two pinches of salt and a couple of twists of the pepper mill. Add the thyme and parsley, the bay leaf, broken into small pieces and the coriander seeds and mix together.

Clean the anchovies carefully, as they are very delicate: cut off the heads and gently squeeze out the intestines without crushing the fish. Pat dry on kitchen paper then lay them on a clean cloth, sprinkle with fine sea salt and leave to stand for 2 hours.

Wash the anchovies under cold running water and pat dry on kitchen paper then arrange them delicately in a white pottery terrine, cover with the lid and set aside.

Transfer the marinade to a saucepan and heat over a high heat. When it comes to the boil, pour over the anchovies. Peel the remaining onion and cut into thin slices. Cut the lemon into thin slices and arrange them with the onion over the anchovies. Leave the anchovies to marinate in the refrigerator for 24 hours.

Just before serving, wash the potatoes and steam them for 10 minutes in their skins. When they are just cooked, run cold water over them then peel, slice into thin rounds and place them in a deep dish. Serve with the anchovies.

Carpaccio of fresh tuna with basil

PREPARATION TIME: 30 MINUTES / NO COOKING REQUIRED

Serves 4

300 g (11 oz) very fresh red tuna
100 ml (3½ fl oz) extra virgin olive oil infused with basil
1 tsp fine sea salt • juice of ½ lime
freshly ground black pepper • 4 basil leaves
8 slices of country-style bread

Skin the tuna and carefully remove all the bones, pat dry on kitchen paper and slice it very finely with a sharp knife or, better still, an electric slicer. To make this easier, place the tuna in the freezer for 15–20 minutes beforehand.

Using a pastry brush, brush four plates with olive oil and lay the slices of tuna on them. Brush the tuna with the rest of the oil then sprinkle with fine salt and moisten with a few drops of lime juice. Season generously with pepper. Place a basil leaf on each plate and serve with toasted slices of country-style bread.

Mackerel rillettes

PREPARATION TIME: 20 MINUTES / COOKING TIME: 20 MINUTES
CHILLING TIME: 24 HOURS / PREPARE THE DAY BEFORE

Serves 4

**200 ml (7 fl oz) Court-bouillon (see page 42) • 500 g (1 lb 2 oz) fine fresh mackerel
2 onions • 3 garlic cloves • salt and freshly ground black pepper
100 ml (3½ fl oz) crème fraîche • ½ bunch of chervil**

Heat the Court-bouillon in a large saucepan over a low heat. Clean the mackerel and remove the heads and tails. Plunge them into the Court-bouillon for 5 minutes then lift them out carefully with a slotted spoon and leave to cool in a colander. Remove the skin and bones and set the flesh aside.

Peel and finely chop the onions and garlic and sweat them in a large saucepan over a very low heat. Add the mackerel flesh, season with salt and pepper and mix well. Add the crème fraîche and allow the mixture to cook over a low heat for 5 minutes.

When it is cooked leave to cool completely then mash with a fork. Finely chop the chervil, leaving a few sprigs for the garnish, and mix into the mixture. Fill small ramekins with the mixture and leave to set in the refrigerator for 24 hours. Garnish with the reserved chervil sprigs and serve with toasted slices of country-style bread.

Salmon with warm potatoes

PREPARATION TIME: 20 MINUTES / COOKING TIME: 10 MINUTES

Serves 4

**200 g (7 oz) firm, waxy potatoes, such as Charlotte or Ratte
sea salt and freshly ground black pepper
1 good fresh salmon fillet weighing about 500 g (1 lb 2 oz)
2 limes · 10 g (¼ oz) fine sea salt · 3 tbsp olive oil
1 small glass dry white wine · 3 white onions**

Wash the potatoes and cook them, still in their skins, in boiling salted water for a good 10 minutes. At the end of that time, test them with a fork and, if they are cooked but still a little firm, take them off the heat and leave to finish cooking in the water while you prepare the salmon.

Remove any residual bones from the salmon fillet with a pair of tweezers then place in the freezer briefly to firm up. This makes the salmon easier to slice.

Meanwhile, prepare the marinade: squeeze the limes and add the salt to the juice (and a little sugar if you wish to soften the acidity of the limes) and mix well. Add the olive oil and whisk thoroughly then set aside until required.

Drain the potatoes and peel, then place the potatoes in a bowl, pour over the white wine and leave to cool until warm.

Pour the marinade into a large, shallow serving dish. Cut the salmon into slices and arrange them in an overlapping layer in the marinade. Leave to stand in a cool place until required.

When the potatoes are just warm, arrange them beside the salmon slices. Peel the onions, slice them into rings and lay them over the potatoes. Season with a few twists of the pepper mill, sprinkle with sea salt and serve immediately with a rocket, onion and carrot salad.

My Tip

I prefer to use a good quality extra-virgin olive oil such as one from Pantelleria. I like to add a little salmon caviar, which gives extra sophistication to the dish.

Mackerel in white wine

Serves 4

500 g (1 lb 2 oz) small mackerel
3 carrots · 3 shallots · 3 black peppercorns
3 juniper berries · 4 coriander seeds · salt
a few herb sprigs (thyme, rosemary, bay leaf)
½ bottle good white wine

Wash and dry the mackerel, cut off the heads and tails, open out the two fillets and remove the backbone. Lay them on kitchen paper.

Peel the carrots and shallots. Roughly chop the shallots and slice the carrots into thin round slices.

Preheat the oven to 180°C/350°F/gas mark 4. Arrange a layer of carrot slices in the base of a white porcelain terrine and cover with a layer of shallots then a layer of mackerel, folded again to their original shape. Cover with another layer of carrots and shallots, then another layer of mackerel until all the ingredients are used, finishing with a carrot and shallot layer. Distribute the peppercorns, juniper berries and coriander seeds evenly over the top then sprinkle with the salt and herbs. Pour over the wine. Cover the dish. Place the terrine in a bain-marie or a large roasting tin and pour in enough boiling water to come halfway up the sides of the terrine and cook in the preheated oven for about 40–45 minutes. The liquid needs to simmer but not boil.

Remove from the oven and leave to cool completely. Serve the mackerel, well chilled, with perhaps a creamy potato salad, or a beetroot salad for example.

My Tip

If you can, choose small, immature mackerel; they have a more delicate, less oily flesh than the larger ones. You could modify this traditional recipe by adding cider to the marinade – in which case do not use wine – or even raspberry vinegar.

Pink bream tartare

PREPARATION TIME 20 MINUTES / NO COOKING REQUIRED

Serves 4

**2 shallots · 1 small bunch of chervil
2 gherkins · 1 tsp capers · 1 egg
1 tsp mustard · a dash of olive oil
fine sea salt and freshly ground black pepper
1 squeeze of lime juice (optional)
a dash of Tabasco sauce (optional)
1 good-sized bream, filleted, about 300 g (11 oz) flesh
125 g (4 oz) purslane · 1 piece of fresh root ginger
a few basil leaves**

Peel and finely chop the shallots. Chop the chervil and mix with the shallots. Finely chop the gherkins and capers and add to the herb and shallot mixture.

Break the egg and separate the white from the yolk. Mix the yolk with the mustard and whisk, gradually drizzling in the olive oil to make a mayonnaise. Season with salt and pepper and add the Tabasco or lime juice, if using.

Roughly chop the fish with a knife so that it keeps all its texture and beautiful pinkish colour.

Mix the fish with the mayonnaise you have just prepared and add the chopped shallot and herbs. Drizzle a little more olive oil over it and mix well.

Strew the purslane salad on large plates. Form the bream 'tartare' into large cork shapes and place them in the centre of the plates. Peel, then grate or finely chop the piece of ginger and sprinkle a little over the fish and, if you like, add a sprinkling of chopped shallot, basil leaves or some finely chopped chervil and serve well chilled.

My Tip

*I also like to make this dish with gilt-head bream,
salmon or bass. In season I add a few scallops,
which have such a melting texture…*

Breton lobster salad

PREPARATION TIME: 50 MINUTES / COOKING TIME: 30 MINUTES

Serves 4

2 litres (3½ pints) Court-bouillon (see page 42)
4 small lobsters, preferably from Brittany, 300–400 g (11–14 oz) each
200 g (7 oz) extra-fine French beans • 1 bunch of chervil
300 g (11 oz) mixed young wild salad leaves or other green salad
100 g (3½ oz) slow-roasted tomatoes
For the vinaigrette 3 tbsp olive oil • 1 tbsp aged wine vinegar
salt and freshly ground black pepper • 2 shallots
1 small piece of fresh root ginger

Bring the Court-bouillon to the boil in a large saucepan. Place the lobsters in the boiling Court-bouillon and leave to cook for 10–15 minutes, according to their size. When the lobsters are cooked, lift them out with a slotted spoon and place them in a colander. Rinse them quickly under cold running water and leave to cool.

Top and tail the French beans and wash them. Steam for 7 minutes then leave to cool.

To prepare the vinaigrette, mix the oil and vinegar together then season with a pinch of salt and a few twists of the pepper mill. Finely chop the shallots and add to the vinaigrette. Wash and dry the chervil and the salad leaves.

When the lobsters are tepid or cold, shred the salad leaves and arrange them on individual serving plates. Carefully take the lobsters out of their shells and cut the body parts into slices. Then reform these body parts onto serving plates. Place the claws on either side of the main body, the head, emptied of its contents at the top, and the tail at the bottom. Add the French beans and drizzle over the vinaigrette.

Using scissors, snip the chervil over the lobsters and garnish with the slow-roasted tomatoes. Serve immediately, either warm or cold.

My Tip

This recipe is a classic one on which to base dishes made with crayfish, langoustines, crabs and other crustaceans…

Meltingly soft crab

PREPARATION TIME: 2 HOURS / COOKING TIME: ABOUT 50 MINUTES

Serves 4

For the Court-bouillon **2 onions • 2 carrots**
1 small celery stick • salt and freshly ground black pepper
1 bouquet garni (thyme, bay leaf, parsley) • 2 tbsp wine vinegar
lemon juice (optional) • 4 fresh whole crabs (preferably female)
1 lemon, cut into quarters
For the vinaigrette **3 tbsp olive oil • 1 tbsp aged wine vinegar**
1 small piece of fresh root ginger

To prepare the Court-bouillon, peel and chop the onions, scrape the carrots and cut into round slices. Place them with the celery stick in a large saucepan, cover with water, add the salt, bouquet garni and vinegar, and bring to the boil. Cook for 20 minutes or so and leave to infuse. Strain the Court-bouillon through a sieve and pour back into the saucepan. You could also add some lemon juice or a little local dry white wine (Muscadet, for example).

Place the crabs in the pan containing the Court-bouillon and cook for 20 minutes. Use two pans if one is not large enough.

When the crabs are cooked, strain off the liquid and leave the crabs to cool in a colander. When the crabs are cool enough to handle, remove the legs and open the shells. Take out all the meat including the brownish part beneath the head. When you have removed all the meat from the legs and bodies of the crabs, even from all the little crevices (a lengthy process), remove the cartilage from the claw meat, keeping the pieces whole and set aside with the emptied shells. Place the crabmeat in a large mixing bowl.

To prepare the vinaigrette, mix the olive oil and vinegar together, season with salt and pepper and add the ginger, peeled and grated. Mix the vinaigrette thoroughly with the crabmeat.

Fill the shells with the crabmeat mixture, place the claw meat on top, garnish with lemon quarters and leave in the refrigerator until required.

Ham with parsley, Burgundy style

PREPARATION TIME: 40 MINUTES / COOKING TIME: 3 HOURS 45 MINUTES
SOAKING TIME: 12 HOURS / CHILLING TIME: 24 HOURS / PREPARE TWO DAYS BEFORE

Serves 4

2 kg (4½ lb) gammon or shoulder ham with rind on • 2 carrots • 1 onion
4 garlic cloves • 1 celery stick • 1 bouquet garni (thyme, parsley, bay leaf)
1 bottle white Burgundy wine • 1 calf's foot
3 shallots • 1 large bunch of flat-leaf parsley
1 bunch of tarragon • 100 ml (3½ fl oz) white wine vinegar
salt and freshly ground black pepper

To remove the excess salt, soak the ham in plenty of cold water for 12 hours, changing the water regularly.

The next day, prepare the stock: peel the carrots, onion, 2 of the garlic cloves and celery and cut into large pieces. Place them in a stockpot with the bouquet garni, white wine and ham. Add enough water to cover then bring to the boil over a high heat and cook for 30 minutes.

At the end of the cooking time, remove any scum that has formed, add the calf's foot, cut in half, and season well with salt and pepper. Make up the quantity with water if needed, cover and simmer over a low heat for 3 hours. By then the meat should come away easily.

Peel and finely chop the shallots and remaining garlic, wash the parsley and tarragon, dry them and chop finely. Take the meats out of the stock, remove the bone from the ham, detach the best pieces of meat, cut them into chunks or strips and roll them in the chopped parsley and tarragon. Remove the meat from the calf's foot and roughly chop, with the ham rind and trimmings. Mix thoroughly with the garlic, shallots and any remaining parsley and tarragon.

Take about 1 litre (1¾ pints) of the stock and strain it through a sieve into a clean saucepan. Add the vinegar and place over a high heat until the liquid is reduced. Leave to cool.

Pour one ladle of the reduced liquor into the base of a terrine or salad bowl, leave to set for a while then arrange a layer of the herb-coated ham chunks or strips and cover with a layer of the chopped meats. Continue adding alternating layers of ham pieces and the chopped meats, pouring in a little of the liquor between each layer and ending with a layer of the chopped meats. Tap the container on the work surface so that the liquor penetrates throughout the whole, then put a little board on top of the terrine with a weight on top and leave to cool in the refrigerator until the next day. The cooking liquor should set to form a jelly.

Cut the ham into slices while still in the terrine and serve with country-style bread.

Terrine Lorraine

PREPARATION TIME: 1 HOUR / COOKING TIME: 1 HOUR 30 MINUTES
SETTING TIME: 24 HOURS / PREPARE THE DAY BEFORE

Serves 4

**500 g (1 lb 2 oz) lean veal • 500 g (1 lb 2 oz) diced hare or rabbit, prepared
by your butcher; with bones • salt and freshly ground black pepper
freshly ground nutmeg • 3 onions • 6 shallots • 1 bunch of parsley
100 g (3½ oz) smoked streaky bacon • 200 g (7 oz) mixed minced meat
40 g (1½ oz) butter • 200 ml (7 fl oz) dry white wine**
For the 'jelly' **1 calf's foot, cut into small pieces by your butcher
1 onion, peeled and studded with 2–3 cloves
1 bouquet garni (bay leaf, parsley, thyme)
700 ml (1¼ pt) dry white wine
salt • crushed black peppercorns**

Preheat the oven to 200°C/400°F/gas mark 6. Dice the veal finely and mix with the hare or rabbit meat. Season generously with salt, pepper and nutmeg.

Peel the onions and shallots and dice finely. Wash the parsley and shake dry, pull off the leaves and chop finely. Cut the bacon into very small pieces. Mix the minced meat with the onions, shallots, parsley and bacon in a large bowl.

Grease a terrine dish generously with the butter. Place alternate layers of diced meat and minced meat mixture into the dish. Pour over the wine and cook uncovered in the preheated oven for about 1¹/₂ hours.

Meanwhile prepare the jelly: place the hare or rabbit bones, the chopped calf's foot, the onion studded with cloves and the bouquet garni in a large pan. Pour in the wine and season with salt and crushed peppercorns. Bring to the boil then leave to simmer.

Remove the terrine from the oven. Strain the jelly through a sieve over the terrine. Cover with a small chopping board or a plate and weigh down with a heavy object. Leave the terrine to solidify in the refrigerator for at least 24 hours.

To serve: carefully transfer the terrine to a long serving dish or, alternatively, serve in the original dish. Serve with fresh, rustic bread or a baguette.

Jellied rabbit

PREPARATION TIME: 1 HOUR / COOKING TIME: 1 HOUR
MARINATING TIME: 12 HOURS / PREPARE THE DAY BEFORE

Serves 4

1 fat rabbit, completely boned and cut into pieces (ask your supplier to do this)
2 onions • 2 carrots • the rabbit bones • 1 calf's foot
100 g (3½ oz) lean bacon in one piece • 1 large bunch of flat-leaf parsley
a few whole chive lengths
For the marinade **½ bottle good quality dry white wine**
1 glass olive oil • 1 bouquet garni (thyme, parsley, bay leaf)
salt and freshly ground black pepper • 2 onions • 2 carrots

Prepare the marinade the day before: place the wine and olive oil in a deep dish with the bouquet garni, and season with salt and pepper. Add the onions and carrots, cut into pieces, and the rabbit pieces including the liver. Mix well and cover with clingfilm or aluminium foil and leave to marinate for 12 hours, turning the pieces from time to time.

The next day, prepare the jelly: peel and roughly chop one onion and one carrot and cook for 1 hour with the rabbit bones and calf's foot. At the end of that time, strain the jelly through a very fine sieve or, preferably, a conical sieve and leave to cool.

Preheat the oven to 200°C/400°F/gas mark 6. Cut the bacon into very thin slices and use to line the base and sides of a terrine. Peel and chop the remaining onion and carrot, fill the terrine with the rabbit pieces, sprinkle the onion and carrot over and add a little of the marinade. Cover and cook in the preheated oven for about 1 hour, making sure the liquid in the terrine does not evaporate completely. If necessary, cook it in a bain-marie or

a large roasting tin filled with enough boiling water to come halfway up the sides of the terrine.

When the rabbit has cooked for about 1 hour, remove from the oven and leave to cool. Wash and finely chop the parsley, reserving a sprig for the garnish, and add to the jelly, which is in the process of setting but should not be solid.

Take out the thighs and the two whole pieces of saddle from the terrine. Chop them roughly with a knife. Leave the rest of the saddle and the liver whole. Pour a little of the jelly into the terrine and set the two whole saddle pieces and the liver into it, then cover with a layer of chopped rabbit. Add further layers of jelly and chopped rabbit until all the ingredients are used up. Tap it on the work surface to tamp it down and add the rest of the jelly, which should completely cover the rabbit. Cover with a lid and leave to cool completely. Refrigerate and wait a day or two before sampling this rabbit 'terrine'. Serve garnished with a parsley sprig and a few whole chives.

Pork brawn

PREPARATION TIME: 1 HOUR / COOKING TIME: 5–8 HOURS
CHILLING TIME: 24–36 HOURS / PREPARE SEVERAL DAYS IN ADVANCE

Serves 4

3 onions · 2 cloves · 4 carrots
2 bouquets garni (thyme, bay leaf, parsley, celery)
1 pig's head · 1 pig's trotter · 1 litre (1¾ pints) dry white wine
salt and freshly ground black pepper · salad leaves

Peel the onions and press a clove into two of them. Peel the carrots and cut into large pieces then place them in a large stockpot. Add the bouquets garni, the pig's head and the trotter, split into two. Pour in the wine, season with salt and pepper and add enough water to cover. Simmer for at least 5 hours and even as long as 8 hours depending on whether the meats are crammed together or have room to move about. Skim the surface regularly with a slotted spoon.

Leave the meats to cool completely before removing them from the cooking liquor. Cut the pig's head into strips, scrape the meat from the trotter and mix all the meats together in a large mixing bowl. Strain the cooking liquor and pour over the meat until it is completely covered. Leave to set into a jelly for 24–36 hours.

To serve, cut the brawn into slices and arrange them on a bed of green salad leaves. Serve with small pickled gherkins.

My Tip

Transform this basic recipe into a festive dish!
While the meats are cooling, add some unsalted
pistachio nuts that have been blanched for
1 minute in boiling water then skinned.
You could also add some chopped garlic,
shallot and flat-leaf parsley.

Ox muzzle with vinaigrette

PREPARATION TIME: 1 HOUR / COOKING TIME: 7 HOURS
CHILLING TIME: 24 HOURS / PREPARE THE DAY BEFORE

Serves 4

3 litres (5¼ pints) water • 1 bouquet garni
3 onions, peeled and a clove studded into two of them
3 carrots • coarse salt • 5 peppercorns
1 ox muzzle ordered from the butcher • 1 calf's foot
For the vinaigrette **3 tbsp groundnut oil • 1 tsp aged wine vinegar**
salt and freshly ground black pepper • ½ tsp wholegrain mustard
½ bunch of flat-leaf parsley • ½ bunch of chervil • ½ bunch of chives

Boil the water with the bouquet garni, 2 onions studded with cloves, 3 carrots, peeled and cut into round slices, coarse salt and the peppercorns. Leave to boil for 20 minutes.

Place the ox muzzle in the boiling water and leave to cook. After 30 minutes, add the calf's foot, split in half, and cook for a further 30 minutes. By this time the muzzle will be scalded and fit to eat. Lift out the muzzle and the calf's foot, carefully strain the cooking liquor, preferably through a conical or fine sieve, then pour it back into the pan over a high heat. Return the meat to the pan, cover and leave to simmer slowly for 5 hours. Skim regularly with a slotted spoon to clear the broth.

At the end of the cooking time the meat should come away easily from the bones; leave it to cool in the cooking liquor.

When the muzzle is cold, cut it into large pieces. Scrape the meat from the halves of calf's foot and mix it with the muzzle in a large terrine. Strain the cooking liquor and pour over the meat. Cover the terrine with a lid and leave to set in the refrigerator for at least 24 hours.

Just before serving, prepare the vinaigrette: whisk the oil and vinegar together. Season with salt and pepper, add the mustard and mix well. Add the chopped parsley, chervil and chives and mix until the herbs are thoroughly incorporated.

To unmould the muzzle, turn the terrine upside down and give it a sharp tap on a clean surface. Cut the muzzle into very thin slices and place them in a salad bowl. Pour the herb vinaigrette over them and serve immediately.

Pressed oxtail with leeks

PREPARATION TIME: 20 MINUTES / COOKING TIME: 2 HOURS
CHILLING TIME: 24 HOURS / PREPARE THE DAY BEFORE

Serves 4

**2 carrots • 2 onions • 2 garlic cloves • 2 bouquets garni
1 kg (2¼ lb) oxtail • 8 baby leeks • 1 tsp powdered gelatine
½ bunch of chervil • 2 tbsp olive oil • salt and freshly ground black pepper**

Peel the carrots, onions and garlic, cut into pieces and place them in a sauté pan. Add the bouquets garni and enough water to cover and bring to the boil. Cut the oxtail into pieces 6–7 cm (2–3 in) long and add them to the pan, cover and cook over a medium heat for about 2 hours, skimming the surface regularly with a slotted spoon.

Peel the leeks and discard the green part, which can be made into leek and potato soup, and steam for 15 minutes.

When the oxtail is well cooked and the meat breaks up easily, lift it out with a slotted spoon, leave to drain then remove the bones and pat dry on kitchen paper.

To make the jelly, strain the cooking liquor through a sieve then pour it into a clean saucepan and heat until it is not quite to boiling point.

Take the pan off the heat, sprinkle in the gelatine and stir vigorously until the gelatine is completely dissolved. Leave to cool slightly.

Pour a little of the jelly into the base of a white porcelain terrine. Tilt it round to make the jelly stick to the sides before placing a layer of oxtail in the base then adding a layer of leeks, continuing like that until all the ingredients are used up – ending with a layer of oxtail. Cover with jelly, place a wooden board on the top, press down and place a weight on the board. Leave to set in the refrigerator for at least 24 hours.

To serve, turn the terrine upside down over a serving dish and give it a sharp tap to unmould the oxtail. Cut the pressed oxtail into slices, garnish with a few sprigs of chervil and drizzle some olive oil over them.

My Tip

Adding half a calf's foot to the oxtail provides the necessary gelatine for the jelly to set when cold, as well as giving extra flavour to the dish. Calf's feet can be ordered from your local butcher.

Peppers marinated in olive oil

PREPARATION TIME: 40 MINUTES / COOKING TIME: 30 MINUTES
MARINATING TIME: 24 HOURS (OPTIONAL) / PREPARE THE DAY BEFORE

Serves 4

**3 red peppers • 3 yellow peppers • 1 garlic bulb
salt and freshly ground black pepper
300 ml (½ pt) extra virgin olive oil • 1 lime**

Preheat the oven to 240°C/475°F/gas mark 9. Wash the peppers and dry them on kitchen paper. Place them in a roasting dish in the preheated oven and let them blacken, turning them from time to time. When they are blackened all over, remove them from the oven and leave to cool.

Peel the garlic and cut into very fine strips. Peel the peppers, cut in half and remove the stem and carefully take out all the seeds. Cut the peppers into long strips and place them in a white porcelain terrine. Season with salt and pepper and sprinkle over a little garlic. Cover with olive oil and some lime juice, cover with a lid and leave to marinate for 24 hours, if possible. Serve very cold with toast.

Leeks with vinaigrette

PREPARATION TIME: 25 MINUTES / COOKING TIME: 20 MINUTES

Serves 4

1 kg (2¼ lb) small, young leeks • 4 eggs
For the vinaigrette **2 shallots • 4 tbsp olive oil • 1 tbsp aged wine vinegar
salt and freshly ground black pepper • 1 bunch of chervil or chives**

Discard the green part of the leeks, wash the white parts and cut them into 10 cm (4 in) lengths. Steam them for about 10 minutes, depending on how thick they are.

While they are cooking, hard-boil the eggs for 9 minutes. Peel and chop the shallots.

To prepare the vinaigrette: mix the oil and vinegar together. Add the chopped shallots, season with salt and pepper and mix well. Using scissors, snip

half of the chervil into the vinaigrette.
When the leeks are cooked, drain them on kitchen paper and leave to cool. Shell the eggs and wash under cold running water.

Arrange the leeks in a serving dish and surround them with two of the eggs, cut into quarters. Roughly chop the remaining eggs and sprinkle them over the leeks then pour over the vinaigrette. Snip the rest of the chervil over the leeks and serve immediately.

Curly endive with bacon lardons

PREPARATION TIME: 10 MINUTES / COOKING TIME: 5 MINUTES

Serves 4

1 good head curly endive with a yellow centre • 200 g (7 oz) lean smoked bacon in one piece
For the mustard sauce **2 shallots • 1 tsp wholegrain mustard • 1 tbsp aged wine vinegar**
salt and freshly ground black pepper • 4 tbsp sunflower oil

Wash the endive carefully, drain and spin dry in a salad spinner. Separate the leaves.

Remove any gristly parts from the bacon and cut into lardons. Blanch these in boiling water then drain and sauté them in a non-stick frying pan.

To prepare the mustard sauce: peel and chop the shallots. Mix the mustard with the vinegar, add the shallots, season with salt and pepper and slowly drizzle in the sunflower oil as you would to make mayonnaise.

Place the endive leaves and the bacon lardons in a large salad bowl, cover with the mustard sauce, mix well using salad servers, and serve immediately with garlic croûtons.

Foie gras in Muscat wine

PREPARATION TIME: 20 MINUTES / COOKING TIME: 20 MINUTES–1 HOUR
MARINATING TIME: 12 HOURS / CHILLING TIME: 24 HOURS / PREPARE TWO DAYS BEFORE

Serves 4

2 foies gras, weighing about 400–500 g (14 oz–1 lb 2 oz) each
salt and freshly ground black pepper • ½ lemon • 1 bottle Muscat wine

Trim and carefully remove all trace of the tubes and filaments from the foies gras. Pat dry on kitchen paper, season with salt and pepper and add a few drops of lemon juice to stop them from darkening. Place the foies gras in a heavy-based casserole and cover with the Muscat wine. Leave to marinate in the refrigerator for 12 hours.

The next day, preheat the oven to 190°C/375°F/gas mark 5. Place the casserole in the oven and cook for about 10 minutes.

At the end of the cooking time, remove the casserole from the oven, transfer the foies gras to an ovenproof earthenware terrine, pour over the wine marinade and return to the oven for a further 10 minutes.

By this time the foies gras should be half-cooked; remove the terrine from the oven and leave to cool completely before storing in the refrigerator until needed – preferably for at least 24 hours, as the foies gras need time to contract and solidify. Serve with slices of toasted country-style bread

My Tip

If you prefer your foie gras cooked through rather than half-cooked as in this recipe, preheat the oven to 110°C/225°F/gas mark ¼. Place the terrine in a bain-marie or large roasting tin filled with enough boiling water to come halfway up the sides of the terrine and cook for 1 hour. Remove from the oven and leave to cool completely then store in the refrigerator.

Eggs 'meurette'

PREPARATION TIME: 30 MINUTES / COOKING TIME: 30 MINUTES

Serves 4

**1 onion • 2 small young carrots • 4 shallots • 4 garlic cloves
500 ml (16 fl oz) French red wine, such as Anjou
1 bouquet garni (thyme, bay leaf, parsley, celery)
salt and freshly ground black pepper • a small sugar cube (optional)
200 g (7 oz) smoked streaky bacon in one piece • 1 slightly stale baguette
8 eggs • 1 bunch of flat-leaf parsley or tarragon**

Peel and roughly chop the onion, carrots and shallots. Peel 3 garlic cloves and cut into fine slices.

Place the red wine in a saucepan and bring to a slow boil. Add the chopped vegetables, bouquet garni and salt and pepper and leave to simmer for about 10 minutes, adding a small sugar cube if necessary to counteract the acidity.

Remove the skin and any gristly parts from the bacon and cut it into thin strips. Place them in a saucepan of cold water and bring to the boil for 3 minutes then drain and set aside until required.

Cut the baguette into round slices and cut off the crusts. Rub the slices on both sides with the remaining garlic, peeled, then cut the slices into small croûtons. Set aside.

Strain the wine sauce through a fine sieve, return to the pan and poach the eggs one by one over a very low heat (about 5 minutes).

Heat four soup plates in boiling water, then dry them and divide the garlic croûtons between them. Place two eggs in the centre of each, pour over the wine sauce and strew with the bacon strips. Sprinkle with chopped flat-leaf parsley or tarragon.

My Tip

If possible, use a red Anjou wine from the Chateau de Tigné.

Scrambled eggs with asparagus tips

PREPARATION TIME: 30 MINUTES / COOKING TIME: 20 MINUTES

Serves 4

2 bunches of asparagus, preferably the green kind
80 g (3 ¼ oz) butter · 8 eggs
salt and freshly ground black pepper
½ stale baguette

Use only the tips of the asparagus and only peel them if necessary. Cook the asparagus in a steamer for about 7 minutes then leave to cool slightly.

Melt 20 g (¾ oz) butter in a frying pan, add the asparagus tips, cover and leave to cook for about 5 minutes, turning them from time to time.

Break the eggs into a bowl and beat them very lightly until they are just mixed. Season with salt and pepper. Melt 20 g (¾ oz) butter in a non-stick sauté pan, pour in the beaten eggs and stir with a wooden spoon. Set the pan in a bain-marie or a large roasting tin filled with enough boiling water to come halfway up the sides of the pan and cook the eggs, stirring constantly, until they start to stick to the walls of the pan. Remove from the heat, cover and set aside.

Cut the baguette into round slices. Melt 30 g (1 oz) butter in a large frying pan and fry the baguette slices for 5 minutes on each side. Cut the rest of the butter into small pieces and stir them into the scrambled eggs, then incorporate the asparagus tips, taking care not to break them up.

Spoon the scrambled eggs and asparagus tips onto warmed plates, surround with the fried baguette slices and serve immediately.

When in season, chanterelle mushrooms may also be used in this recipe instead of the asparagus.

My Tip

For a festive occasion, add a small black or white truffle, cut into fine strips.

Quiche Lorraine

PREPARATION TIME: 20 MINUTES / COOKING TIME: 30 MINUTES
CHILLING TIME: 12 HOURS / PREPARE THE DAY BEFORE

Serves 4

10 g (¼ oz) butter • **4 good-sized onions** • **250 g (9 oz) smoked streaky bacon, in one piece**
100 g (3 ½ oz) Comté or Emmental cheese • **5 eggs** • **100 g (3½ oz) thick crème fraîche**
500 ml (16 fl oz) milk • **salt and freshly ground black pepper** • **a pinch of nutmeg**
For the shortcrust pastry **250 g (9 oz) sifted plain flour, plus extra to dust**
a pinch of salt • **1 egg** • **140 g (4½ oz) softened butter** • **200 ml (7 fl oz) water**

Prepare the pastry the day before: place the flour and salt in a mixing bowl, make a well in the centre and break the egg into it. Add the butter, cut into small pieces and mix with your fingertips, adding the water a little at a time until the mixture forms a slightly elastic dough. Roll into a ball and wrap in clingfilm then leave in the refrigerator for 12 hours.

The next day, preheat the oven to 180°C/350°F/ gas mark 4. Grease a fairly deep round tart tin with the butter.

Unwrap the pastry and place on a large, lightly floured work surface. Roll the pastry out and use to line the base and sides of the prepared tart tin. Bake blind (lined with greaseproof paper weighted with dried beans) for about 10 minutes.

Meanwhile, prepare the filling: peel and roughly chop the onions. Cut off the rind from the bacon then cut it into lardons and blanch in a pan of boiling water for 5 minutes, then drain. Grate the cheese on a coarse grater.

Sweat the onions in a large, non-stick frying pan and when they have become transparent add the bacon lardons and leave to sizzle for 5 minutes.

Beat the eggs, crème fraîche, milk, half the grated cheese, salt, pepper and nutmeg together in a mixing bowl. Add the onions and bacon and mix thoroughly.

Remove the pastry case from the oven, take out the paper and dried beans and pour in the egg mixture. Sprinkle over the rest of the cheese and return to the oven for about 20 minutes. The top should be golden brown and crisp, but the centre must remain soft.

My Tip

I like my Quiche Lorraine with onions but the authentic recipe does not contain them. I wonder what you think…

Ravioli filled with langoustines and flat-leaf parsley

PREPARATION TIME: 30 MINUTES / COOKING TIME: 1 MINUTE

Serves 4

**16 small fresh langoustines · 1 bunch of flat-leaf parsley
1 packet of wonton wrappers from a Chinese grocer's · 1 egg yolk, beaten
salt · 50 g (2 oz) butter · ½ lemon, preferably organic or one from Menton**

Shell the langoustines and remove the heads and tails. Wash the parsley and dry it on kitchen paper, then pull off the leaves in little sprigs, reserving a few for the garnish.

Lay 16 squares of wonton wrappers out on a work surface and place 2 parsley sprigs and a langoustine in the centre of each. Cover with 2 more parsley sprigs then lay a second square of pastry on top of

each, sticking them together with beaten egg yolk. Trim the ravioli to whatever shape you like with a knife.

Cook the ravioli in plenty of boiling salted water for 1 minute. Drain carefully and coat with melted butter and a touch of lemon juice. Serve immediately while they are piping hot, garnished with parsley sprigs.

Snails in parsley butter

PREPARATION TIME: 15 MINUTES / COOKING TIME: 20 MINUTES

Serves 4

**24 snails, preferably from Burgundy or 24 'petits gris' (another variety), already cooked in brine
salt and freshly ground black pepper • 100 g (3½ oz) fresh butter • 2 garlic cloves
1 bunch of flat-leaf parsley**

To cook the snails, bring a saucepan of salted water to the boil, drop in the snails and blanch for about 10 minutes.

Drain them in a colander and leave to cool while you prepare the parsley butter. Work the butter with a fork until soft then add the garlic, peeled and crushed in a mortar, and the parsley, finely chopped. Season with salt and pepper and mix well to form a well-seasoned creamy paste.

Carefully remove the snails from their shells and discard the black extremity, which makes them taste bitter, then place them back in their shells and add some of the butter you have just prepared. Arrange them in a frying pan and cook until the butter just begins to simmer.

Place them on soup plates, set in a layer of coarse salt to keep them from toppling over. Serve with a good, fresh baguette.

SOUPS AND ONE-POT MEALS

*I adore dishes that stew away gently for hours and, of them all,
soup is my favourite. Soup has always been the traditional family
meal and it is fascinating to see how many different varieties exist
in France alone – from vegetable soups such as Farmer's soup,
whose flavours vary with the ingredients used, to the fish-based,
such as Bouillabaisse from Provence, served with a 'rouille' sauce.
Soup is always a treat.*

Minestrone

PREPARATION TIME: 1 HOUR / COOKING TIME: 1 HOUR
SOAKING TIME: 12 HOURS / PREPARE THE DAY BEFORE

Serves 4

200 g (7 oz) dried haricot beans, such as coco or tarbais beans
3 garlic cloves • 1 celery stick • 2 courgettes • 2 carrots
4 tomatoes • 1 red pepper • 200 g (7 oz) fresh broad beans
1 litre (1¾ pints) water • 200 g (7 oz) fresh garden peas
1 bouquet garni (thyme, bay leaf, parsley)
1 fresh rosemary sprig • salt and freshly ground black pepper
50 g (2 oz) dried rigati or other small pasta shapes • 8 basil leaves • olive oil

Soak the dried beans in plenty of cold water for 12 hours.

The next day, peel the garlic and pound in a mortar. De-string the celery and chop into small cubes. Wash the courgettes, leaving the skin on, and dice them. Scrape and dice the carrots. Wash and dice the tomatoes. Wash the pepper, remove the stem and seeds and cut into cubes.

Drain the soaked beans and rinse them under cold running water. Pod the broad beans and peas. Boil the soaked beans and broad beans in the 1 litre (1¾ pints) of water for about 30 minutes. After 15 minutes add the peas and diced pepper.

At the end of the cooking time, place all the remaining diced vegetables in the saucepan, add the bouquet garni and rosemary and season with salt and pepper. Cover and simmer slowly for a further 30 minutes.

Meanwhile, cook the pasta in a large saucepan of boiling salted water for 7 minutes then drain.

Take the bouquet garni and rosemary out of the soup and discard, add the pasta and leave to cook for a further 5 minutes.

Ladle the minestrone into warmed soup plates, scatter chopped basil leaves over and drizzle over a little olive oil.

My Tip

Place croûtons, freshly grated Parmesan cheese, pesto and tapenade on the table for optional use.

Cream of green asparagus with sorrel

PREPARATION TIME: 30 MINUTES / COOKING TIME: 2 HOURS 15 MINUTES

Serves 4

1 kg (2¼ lb) green asparagus
1 bunch of onions, preferably just pulled, about 150 g (5 oz) total weight
50 ml (2 fl oz) olive oil · 100 ml (3½ fl oz) crème fraîche
50 g (2 oz) butter · 50 g (2 oz) sorrel
For the chicken stock **500 g (1 lb 2 oz) chicken carcasses and giblets**
100 g (3½ oz) carrots · 100 g (3½ oz) onions · 100 g (3½ oz) leeks, white part only
100 g (3½ oz) celery · 1 bouquet garni (thyme, parsley, bay leaf)
salt and freshly ground black pepper

To prepare the chicken stock: place the carcasses and giblets in a stockpot, cover with cold water and bring to the boil. Skim regularly with a slotted spoon and top up with water as you remove the scum that forms on the surface. Skim off any fat.

Peel all the vegetables, cut them into small pieces and add to the stockpot together with the bouquet garni. Season with salt and pepper and leave to cook for 1–2 hours, skimming regularly.

At the end of the cooking time, lift out the chicken carcasses and giblets with a slotted spoon and leave the stock to cool. Strain through a conical or fine sieve and store in bottles for future use.

Peel the asparagus and cut into pieces, keeping the tips for the garnish. Peel and chop the onions, weigh out 150 g (5 oz) and set aside.

Heat half the olive oil in a saucepan and lightly soften the onions, then pour on 1 litre (1¾ pints) of the chicken stock, add the asparagus (without the tips) and cook for 10 minutes.

Pour the mixture into a blender or food processor and blend to a smooth, velvety texture. Cool it quickly on crushed ice.

While it is cooling, whip the crème fraîche with an electric mixer until it emulsifies but is not quite whipped cream.

Melt 20 g (¾ oz) of the butter in a small saucepan and add the sorrel. Stir well with a wooden spoon until it has softened completely.

Reheat the asparagus cream, add the sorrel and whisk vigorously then taste it and adjust the seasoning. Add the asparagus tips and leave to cook gently, without boiling. Add the rest of the butter, cut into small pieces.

Pour this soup into a warmed tureen, drizzle a little of the reserved olive oil over and gently place a rounded spoonful of the emulsified cream in the centre. Serve immediately.

Cream of artichokes with chestnuts

PREPARATION TIME: 1 HOUR / COOKING TIME: 30 MINUTES–1 HOUR

Serves 4

8 small purple artichokes · salt and freshly ground black pepper
60 g (2¼ oz) butter · 500 ml (16 fl oz) milk · 80 g (3¼ oz) crème fraîche
250 g (9 oz) jar of chestnuts in brine

Cook the artichokes in plenty of salted water for about 15 minutes in a pressure cooker. When the artichokes are ready, drain, strip away the leaves and remove the choke. Cut the bases into fine strips and place them in a large saucepan with the butter, milk and half the crème fraîche. Season with salt and pepper, cover and simmer for 15 minutes.

When the artichokes are cooked, pour the contents of the pan into a blender or food processor and blend to a smooth cream. Strain the cream through a conical or fine sieve back into the saucepan and reheat gently. Add the rest of the crème fraîche.

Meanwhile, gently heat the chestnuts in a non-stick frying pan.

To serve, pour the soup into a warmed tureen and scatter the chestnuts over it.

Pink garlic soup

PREPARATION TIME: 20 MINUTES / COOKING TIME: 1 HOUR

Serves 4

12 pink garlic cloves • 2 potatoes • 1 onion
50 g (2 oz) lightly salted butter • 2 glasses Chicken Stock (see page 66)
2 glasses Veal Stock (see page 79) • 1 bouquet garni (thyme, bay leaf, parsley)
100 ml (3½ fl oz) olive oil • 1 stale baguette • ½ bunch of chervil (optional)

Peel the garlic and cut in half. Peel the potatoes and onion and cut into small pieces.

Melt 20 g (¾ oz) of the butter in a large saucepan and gently fry the onion, stirring frequently, for 10 minutes without letting it brown. Add the garlic and potatoes, the Chicken and Veal Stock and the bouquet garni. Bring to the boil then cover and leave to cook for 45 minutes. Add a little water if necessary.

At the end of the cooking time, discard the bouquet garni, remove the garlic with a slotted spoon and crush it thoroughly then return it to the pan and stir well.

Pour the soup into a blender or food processor and blend to a creamy consistency. Strain the soup through a conical or fine sieve, return to the saucepan and reheat. Drizzle in a little olive oil, using a whisk to incorporate it into the soup.

Just before serving, prepare some croûtons: cut the baguette into round slices, cut off the crusts then cut the slices into small cubes and fry them in the remaining butter.

Pour the soup into a warmed tureen and scatter the croûtons over the top. You could also snip some chervil over the soup at the last minute.

Serve immediately, piping hot.

My Tip

As well as having a particularly delicate flavour, this garlic soup is recommended for people suffering from cardiovascular and respiratory problems.

Broad bean soup

PREPARATION TIME: 30 MINUTES / COOKING TIME: 1 HOUR

Serves 4

600 g (1¼ lb) fresh broad beans · 2 shallots · 1 potato
1 litres (1¾ pints) water · 1 sage leaf · 1 savory sprig
salt and freshly ground black pepper
100 g (3½ oz) crème fraîche
½ bunch of basil · 1 bunch of chives

Shell the broad beans, blanch them for 1 minute in a saucepan of boiling water then drain and pop the broad beans out of their skins.

Peel and chop the shallots then peel and dice the potato.

To make the stock: pour the water into a large saucepan, add the sage leaf, savory and salt and pepper. Bring to the boil then add the broad beans and cook for 1 hour.

After 30 minutes, add the potato and shallot and simmer for a further 30 minutes over a low heat.

When the broad beans are cooked, strain the soup through a sieve and set aside one quarter of the beans in a bowl. Place the rest of the beans in a blender, add some of the cooking liquor and blend to a smooth, creamy soup. Gradually add more of the liquid until it reaches the required consistency.

Pour the soup into a clean saucepan, add the crème fraîche and basil and reheat gently. When it is piping hot, ladle into warmed soup plates, scatter the reserved broad beans and snip some chives over the top.

My Tip

Instead of chives you could use chervil or flat-leaf parsley. At the last moment I sometimes add a little diced smoked streaky bacon to this soup.

Tomato and pumpkin soup

PREPARATION TIME: 30 MINUTES / COOKING TIME: 30 MINUTES

Serves 4

500 g (1 lb 2 oz) well-ripened pumpkin · 2 potatoes
2 leeks · 4 tomatoes · 20 g (¾ oz) butter
salt and freshly ground black pepper
200 ml (7 fl oz) crème fraîche
nutmeg · 16 croûtons rubbed with 1 garlic clove
20 g (¾ oz) Parmesan cheese shavings

Peel the pumpkin and cut the flesh into 2 cm (¾ in) cubes. Peel the potatoes, wash and cut them into pieces. Wash the leeks and chop them very small. Wash the tomatoes and blanch them in boiling water for 1 minute then peel, discard the seeds and roughly mash the pulp.

In a large frying pan, soften the chopped leek in the butter, add the tomatoes and cook until they form a creamy sauce. Add the pumpkin and potatoes and enough water to just cover, season with salt and pepper, then cover and leave to simmer for a good 20 minutes.

When the pumpkin is cooked, pour the contents of the pan into a blender or food processor and blend to a creamy, velvety texture.

Pour the soup into a clean saucepan, stir in half the crème fraîche, taste and adjust the seasoning then add a pinch of nutmeg and the rest of the crème fraîche. Reheat gently over a low heat.

When the soup is hot, stir, then serve immediately with croûtons and sprinkled with shavings of Parmesan cheese.

My Tip

I use Reggiano Parmesan cheese, which is very full-flavoured.

Farmer's soup

PREPARATION TIME: 30 MINUTES / COOKING TIME: 30 MINUTES

Serves 4

**½ Savoy cabbage • ½ celeriac • 1 celery stick • 2 good-sized carrots
2 leeks • 2 potatoes • 1 onion • 50 g (2 oz) butter • salt and freshly ground black pepper
2 good slices smoked bacon**

Wash and finely shred the cabbage then drop into a saucepan of boiling salted water and cook for 5 minutes. Peel all the vegetables, wash and cut them into small pieces.

Drain the cabbage in a colander. Melt 20 g (³/₄ oz) butter in a large saucepan, add all the vegetables, cover with water and season with salt and pepper. Cover with a lid and leave to simmer for 30 minutes, adding more water if necessary.

Remove any gristly parts from the bacon and cut it into lardons. Blanch in boiling water then drain and brown the lardons lightly in a non-stick frying pan. Set aside.

When the soup is cooked, spoon the vegetables into soup plates with a slotted spoon. Scatter with the rest of the butter, cut into hazelnut-sized pieces, and the bacon lardons, then ladle on the liquid and serve immediately.

Pesto soup

PREPARATION TIME: 20 MINUTES / COOKING TIME: 50 MINUTES
SOAKING TIME: 12 HOURS (OPTIONAL) / PREPARE THE DAY BEFORE (OPTIONAL)

Serves 4

**200 g (7 oz) fresh white haricot beans or 80 g (3¼ oz) dried haricot beans
1 sage leaf · 1 savory sprig · 1 potato · 2 carrots
2 courgettes · 100 g (3½ oz) French beans · 3 onions
2 celery sticks · 2 tomatoes · salt and freshly ground black pepper
4 slices of country-style bread · 1 bunch of basil
100 ml (3½ fl oz) olive oil**

If you are using dried beans, soak in plenty of cold water for 12 hours. If using fresh ones, shell and soak them in a bowl of cold water.

Cook the beans, sage and savory in a large saucepan for about 30 minutes.

Peel all the vegetables except the tomatoes and cut into small pieces.

Blanch the tomatoes in boiling water, drain, peel and deseed them, then cut them into small cubes. Set aside until required.

Bring a large saucepan of water to the boil and add all the vegetables except the potato. Season with salt and pepper and leave to simmer for 15 minutes. Cook the potato in a separate pan of boiling salted water for 10 minutes then add the beans and cook for a further 10 minutes. When all the vegetables are cooked, transfer to a warmed soup tureen and pour some of their cooking liquor over them.

Toast the slices of bread. Snip the basil finely over the soup, add the tomatoes, drizzle over the olive oil and serve immediately with the toasted bread.

My Tip

*You might serve a pesto sauce or a tapenade
separately with this soup.*

Cream of lentil soup with langoustines and rosemary

PREPARATION TIME: 20 MINUTES / COOKING TIME: 30 MINUTES
SOAKING TIME: 8 HOURS / PREPARE THE DAY BEFORE

Serves 4

250 g (9 oz) Puy lentils · 2 onions · 1 carrot
1 small piece of celeriac · 500 ml (16 fl oz) Chicken Stock (see page 66)
2 rosemary sprigs · 1 slice of good smoked bacon · 1 ham bone
salt and freshly ground black pepper · 1 tbsp crème fraîche
12 fresh langoustines · 2 tbsp olive oil · 4 slow-roasted tomatoes

The day before, sort and wash the lentils and leave to soak in a bowl of cold water overnight.

The next day, peel the onions, carrot and celeriac.

Drain the lentils. Heat the Chicken Stock and one rosemary sprig in a large saucepan. Add the lentils and the slice of bacon, the ham bone and the vegetables, cut into pieces. Season with salt and pepper, cover and leave to cook for 25–30 minutes.

At the end of the cooking time, drain the lentils, discard the rosemary, take out the ham bone and bacon and place the lentils in a blender or food processor. Add the crème fraîche and some of the cooking liquor and blend to a smooth, velvety texture. Add more cooking liquor a little at a time until the soup has reached the required consistency.

Just before serving, cut the bacon into small pieces, sauté them in a dry frying pan and add them to the soup. Shell the langoustines, removing the black thread of intestine, and cook in the olive oil for 7 minutes then drain.

Pour the soup into a clean saucepan and reheat gently over a low heat until hot. Ladle the soup into warmed soup plates, add the langoustines and garnish with the remaining rosemary and the slow-roasted tomatoes.

My Tip

If you wish, before serving the cream of lentil soup you could strain it through a conical or fine sieve to make it even smoother.

Mussel soup with saffron

PREPARATION TIME: 30 MINUTES / COOKING TIME: 30 MINUTES

Serves 4

3 litres (5¼ pints) fresh rope-grown mussels • 200 g (7 oz) firm potatoes
½ glass white wine • 800 ml (1⅓ pints) Chicken Stock (see page 66)
2 onions • generous pinch of powdered saffron • 1 thyme sprig
salt and freshly ground black pepper • 1 tbsp cornflour
200 g (7 oz) crème fraîche • 1 flat-leaf parsley sprig

Clean the mussels, scraping them if necessary, and pull off the beards, then wash well in cold water and drain. Discard any mussels with broken shells or any that refuse to close when tapped.

Peel and dice the potatoes.

Place the mussels in a large saucepan over a very high heat, cover tightly and cook, shaking occasionally, until they have all opened. Discard any mussels that remain closed. Shell the mussels, keeping a few on the half-shell for garnishing, and strain the liquid left in the pan.

Cook the potatoes in a little white wine together with the liquid from the mussels in a separate pan. After 10 minutes, cover the pan then take off the heat and keep hot.

Pour the Chicken Stock into a clean saucepan, add the mussels, potatoes, onions, peeled and finely chopped, and heat. Then add the saffron, thyme and salt and pepper. When it is very hot, transfer the mixture to a blender with the cornflour, add half the crème fraîche and blend to form a creamy, velvety soup.

Pour the soup back into the saucepan and reheat gently.

Just before serving, beat the rest of the crème fraîche until it is just stiff enough to be formed with a spoon and place in the centre of the soup. Serve garnished with a parsley sprig and the reserved mussels.

My Tip

If possible, use mussels grown in the mussel beds around the Mont St Michel.

Bouillabaisse

PREPARATION TIME: 1 HOUR / COOKING TIME: 1 HOUR 30 MINUTES

Serves 4

2 kg (4½ lb) fish caught among the rocks, such as rascasse (scorpion fish), monkfish, cod,
John Dory, sole, red mullet, weever, sea snails, or mussels from Bouzigues
2 onions • 3 garlic cloves • 100 ml (3½ fl oz) olive oil
4 tomatoes • salt and freshly ground black pepper
1 bouquet garni (thyme, bay leaf, parsley) • 2 sage leaves
1 head of fennel • 1 kg (2¼ lb) firm waxy potatoes, such as Charlotte or Ratte
generous pinch of powdered saffron • 4 langoustines • a little Court-bouillon (see page 42)
bread for croutons • 1 star anise
For the rouille sauce **2 garlic cloves • ½ bird's eye chilli (optional)**
1 small cooked potato • a pinch of powdered saffron
200 ml (7 fl oz) olive oil

Gut and meticulously scale the fish, cut off their gills and wash them under cold running water. Cut them into slices or chunks, according to their size and shape, and leave to drain on kitchen paper.

Peel the onions and garlic and roughly chop them. In a heavy-based saucepan, heat 2 tablespoons olive oil and sweat the onions and garlic until they are transparent. Add the pieces of fish and leave to cook over a low heat.

Meanwhile, blanch the tomatoes in boiling water, peel and remove the seeds. Cut the tomatoes into small pieces and add to the saucepan. Cook for a further 5 minutes. Pour on just enough water to cover the fish, season with salt and pepper, add the bouquet garni and sage, and leave to cook over a fairly high heat for at least 30 minutes.

Meanwhile, peel the potatoes and roughly chop. Wash the fennel, cut it into fine slices and fry in

1 tablespoon of olive oil. When they are lightly browned, strain the cooking liquor from the fish through a fine sieve on to the fennel. Bring to the boil, add the fish, saffron and potatoes and leave to cook for a further 10 minutes.

To prepare the rouille sauce: pound the garlic and chilli, if using, in a mortar. Add the potato, mashed, and the saffron then slowly drizzle in the remaining olive oil, mixing vigorously, as when making mayonnaise.

Cut the bread into croûtons and toast in a dry frying pan. Cover the langoustines in Court-bouillon and simmer for 10 minutes.

Pour the bouillabaisse into a large, deep dish, and garnish with the langoustines and star anise. Serve the rouille sauce and croûtons separately.

Cassoulet

PREPARATION TIME: 1 HOUR / COOKING TIME: 3 HOURS
SOAKING TIME: 12 HOURS / PREPARE THE DAY BEFORE

Serves 4

500 g (1 lb 2 oz) dried haricot beans, such as tarbais beans
1 bouquet garni · 1 carrot · 1 onion · 1 clove · 1 garlic clove
100 g (3½ oz) pork rind · salt and freshly ground black pepper
For the meats **80 g (3¼ oz) goose fat, lard or sunflower oil**
1 pork hock (or spare ribs) · 200 g (7 oz) fat bacon in one piece
4 Toulouse sausages · 1 can preserved goose · 3 carrots · 1 onion
1 garlic clove · 1 carton passata (optional) · 3 slices of bread from a tin loaf

Soak the haricot beans in plenty of cold water. Stir from time to time and change the water regularly.

The next day, drain the beans, place them in a large saucepan, cover with cold water, add the bouquet garni, the carrot, peeled and cut into pieces, the onion, peeled with a clove studded into it, the garlic and the pork rind. Season with salt and pepper, bring to the boil and cook for about 1 hour 30 minutes. If you have a pressure cooker then 40 minutes will be enough. At the end of the cooking time, drain the beans but reserve half of the cooking water.

In a large, heavy-based saucepan or stockpot, melt the goose fat, lard or sunflower oil. Cut the meats into sizeable pieces and brown them on all sides in the pan. Prick the sausages with a fork then add them to the pan. When everything is browned, add the preserved goose.

While the meats are cooking, peel the carrots, onion and garlic. Chop them all finely and add to the meat in the stew pot. Add a little passata if using, then the haricot beans and just enough reserved water to cover. Add the lid and leave to stew for 1 hour.

Preheat the oven to 220°C/425°F/gas mark 7. Line a large, ovenproof earthenware casserole with the pork rind, cut into thin slices. Lift the meats out of the pan with a slotted spoon and arrange them in the casserole, alternating layers of meat with layers of beans. Add a little passata and moisten with the cooking liquor from the meats.

Cut the crusts off the loaf and cut it into chunks. Transfer to a food processor and process until fine white breadcrumbs form. Sprinkle the breadcrumbs over the dish and cook in a very hot oven to brown for about 30 minutes. Serve straight from the casserole.

Capon 'cooked in the pot'

PREPARATION TIME: 1 HOUR / COOKING TIME: 3–4 HOURS

Serves 4

1 truffle (optional) • 1 fat capon, preferably one from Bresse
2 leeks • 1 bunch of baby carrots • 1 bunch of small baby turnips
2 purple artichokes • 1 bunch of winter asparagus
20 g (¾ oz) fine sea salt
For the veal stock **1 kg (2¼ lb) veal bones • 100 g (3½ oz) carrots**
100 g (3½ oz) onions • 100 g (3½ oz) leeks, white part only
100 g (3½ oz) celery • 1 bouquet garni (thyme, bay leaf, parsley)
salt and freshly ground black pepper

To prepare the veal stock: roughly chop the bones, or ask your butcher to do it. Place them in a stockpot, cover with cold water and bring to the boil, skimming the surface regularly and topping up the water lost as you remove the scum that forms on the top. Skim off any fat from the surface. Peel and chop the vegetables finely and add to the stockpot together with the bouquet garni. Stir and leave to cook for 3 hours, still skimming regularly. At the end of the cooking time, lift out the bones with the slotted spoon and leave the stock to cool, then pass it through a conical or fine sieve.

If you are using black truffle, cut it into fine slices and insert them under the skin of the bird. This is done by making a small slit and carefully lifting the skin then sliding in the truffle and pressing the skin back again.

Poach the capon in the veal stock, leaving it to simmer slowly for about 1 hour 30 minutes. Meanwhile, peel and cut the leeks, carrots, turnips, artichokes and asparagus into pieces and add to the pan for the last 15 minutes of the cooking time.

When the bird is ready (the legs and wings should come away easily in the hand), transfer the capon to a serving dish and keep hot. Remove the vegetables with a slotted spoon and arrange them around the bird.

Serve the Bresse capon surrounded by vegetables and sprinkled with sea salt. Place the rest of the sea salt in a bowl on the table.

My Tip

The truffle is a refined addition but not indispensable.

Wild rabbit stew with fresh pasta

PREPARATION TIME: 40 MINUTES / COOKING TIME: 2 HOURS
MARINATING TIME: 12 HOURS / PREPARE THE DAY BEFORE

Serves 4

2 shallots • 1 onion • 2 garlic cloves • 2 carrots
1 litre (1¾ pints) French red wine, such as Anjou • 1 bouquet garni (thyme, bay leaf, parsley)
3 juniper berries • 5 tbsp olive oil • 100 ml (3½ fl oz) rabbit's blood
1 small glass of brandy, preferably Cognac • salt and freshly ground black pepper
1 fat rabbit, preferably wild • 200 g (7 oz) streaky bacon in one piece
100 ml (3½ fl oz) crème fraîche
To serve 500 g (1 lb 2 oz) fresh pasta • 1 tbsp olive oil

To prepare the marinade: peel and finely chop the shallots, onion, garlic and carrots. Pour the red wine into a deep dish, add the chopped vegetables, the bouquet garni, the juniper berries, 2 tbsp olive oil, the rabbit's blood and the brandy. Season with salt and pepper and mix well.

Cut the rabbit into pieces and place them in the marinade, cover with clingfilm and leave to marinate in the refrigerator for 12 hours, turning the rabbit pieces from time to time.

The next day, cut the bacon into cubes. Heat the remaining olive oil in a large, cast-iron casserole and brown the bacon and rabbit pieces on all sides. Lift the vegetables out of the marinade with a slotted spoon, then strain the liquid through a sieve and add it to the casserole. Add the vegetables then cover and cook for 2 hours. Just before the end of the cooking time, stir in the crème fraîche.

Five minutes before serving, bring a large saucepan of salted water to the boil. Add 1 tbsp olive oil and add the pasta. Return to the boil and cook for 3 minutes until the pasta is *al dente* (still a little firm to the bite). Drain and transfer to a warmed, deep dish, place the rabbit pieces on top and keep hot.

Strain the rabbit cooking liquor through a fine sieve and pour it over the dish. Serve very hot.

My Tip

At the last moment you could add a little piece of foie gras to the sauce and let it melt before pouring it over the rabbit and pasta.

Pigeon pot-au-feu

PREPARATION TIME: 30 MINUTES / COOKING TIME: 50 MINUTES

Serves 4

4 baby carrots • 1 turnip • 2 leeks • 2 celery sticks
1 litre (1¾ pints) Chicken Stock (see page 66) • 4 pigeons
salt and freshly ground black pepper

Prepare the vegetables: scrape the carrots, peel the turnip and leeks, and de-string the celery. Cut them all into large pieces.

Pour the Chicken Stock into a large saucepan and bring to the boil, then add the pigeons and cook for about 30 minutes.

Add all the vegetables, season with salt and pepper and cook for a further 15 minutes.

Cut the pigeons in half and lay them in a warmed soup tureen. Remove the vegetables with a slotted spoon and arrange them around the half-pigeons. Pour the very hot stock over and serve immediately.

Sauerkraut

PREPARATION TIME: 1 HOUR / COOKING TIME: 2 HOURS

Serves 4

**2 kg (4½ lb) raw sauerkraut • 2 onions • 2 carrots • lard or goose fat
1 bottle Alsatian white wine, such as Sylvaner, Riesling, Gewürztraminer, etc.
2 apples • 6 juniper berries • 1 bouquet garni (thyme, celery, bay leaf, parsley)
salt and freshly ground black pepper • 500 g (1 lb 2 oz) smoked streaky bacon in one piece
4 Strasbourg sausages or other spicy sausage • 1 lightly salted knuckle of ham
1 Morteau sausage or other spicy sausage • 6 potatoes • 4 pork chops**

Preheat the oven to 180°C/350°F/gas mark 4. Wash the sauerkraut very thoroughly, teasing it out between the hands to separate it, run it briefly under cold running water then drain it.

Peel and finely chop the onion and carrots. Melt the lard or goose fat in a large, cast-iron casserole and fry the onions and carrots. Add the sauerkraut and mix well then add a glass of white wine. Cover and heat gently until hot.

Meanwhile, peel the apples and cut them into large pieces. Tie the juniper berries in a piece of muslin and add them to the sauerkraut, together with the bouquet garni, salt, pepper and the smoked bacon. Pour in the rest of the wine, cover and when it comes to the boil, cook in the oven for about 1 hour, making sure that the liquid in the casserole does not dry out.

Bring a saucepan of water to the boil and add the Strasbourg sausages, the knuckle of ham and the Morteau sausage. Return to the boil and cook for 1 hour.

Peel the potatoes, cut them into pieces and add to the sauerkraut after 30 minutes of cooking time.

Meanwhile, preheat the grill. Cook the pork chops without added fat under the hot grill then arrange them on top of the sauerkraut 15 minutes before serving. Drain the Strasbourg sausages, the ham knuckle and the Morteau sausage. Cut the latter into slices and add all the meats to the sauerkraut.

When ready to serve, transfer the sauerkraut to a warmed deep serving dish and surround it with the bacon, the chops, the sausages and the slices of Morteau sausage. Add the potatoes and serve hot.

My Tip

Serve the same kind of wine with the sauerkraut that was used in the cooking.

Salt pork with lentils

PREPARATION TIME: 40 MINUTES / COOKING TIME: 2 HOURS
SOAKING TIME: 3 HOURS

Serves 4

1 kg (2¼ lb) salt pork (knuckle or shoulder) • 1 onion, peeled and studded with a clove
1 bouquet garni • peppercorns • 3 carrots • 1 celery stick • 2 garlic cloves
500 g (1 lb 2 oz) lentils • 30 g (1 oz) butter • 100 g (3½ oz) pork rind
100 g (3½ oz) streaky bacon, cut into lardons
4 good quality sausages, such as Montbéliard • 2 tbsp goose fat

To draw out the salt, soak the salt pork in cold water for 3 hours, changing the water regularly.

Wash the meat under cold running water then place it in a large saucepan with just enough water to cover. Add the onion studded with the clove, the bouquet garni, peppercorns, the carrots, scraped, the celery and the whole garlic cloves, peeled. Leave to simmer for about 1 hour.

Place the lentils in a large saucepan, cover with water, add the butter and bring to simmering point. Leave to cook for 20–25 minutes. When cooked, drain and reserve the cooking water.

Drain the salt pork and discard the stock.

Boil the pork rind and dry it on kitchen paper.

In a large, cast-iron casserole, fry the bacon lardons until they sizzle, add the pork rind, a layer of lentils, then the meat, the sausages, the rest of the lentils, the reserved cooking water and the goose fat. Cover and leave to simmer for about 1 hour.

When it is cooked, remove the meat with a slotted spoon and cut it into slices.

To serve, transfer the lentils to a warmed, deep serving dish and arrange the slices of meat and the sausages on top.

My Tip

I recommend using Puy lentils because they are reputed to have the best flavour. Be careful when cooking – lentils need to cook slowly or they will burst.

Navarin of milk-fed spring lamb with basil

PREPARATION TIME: 35 MINUTES / COOKING TIME: 1 HOUR 10 MINUTES

Serves 4

1. 5 kg (3¼ lb) boned shoulder of milk-fed lamb • 2 tbsp olive oil
1 bunch of basil • 2 garlic cloves • 1 bunch of small white onions, preferably just pulled
200 g (7 oz) tiny garden peas • 200 g (7 oz) very small broad beans
200 g (7 oz) extra-fine French beans • 4 small baby carrots • 2 small baby turnips
1 bunch of green asparagus • 3 purple artichokes • 4 small tomatoes
1 glass Veal Stock (see page 79) • salt and freshly ground black pepper
1 bouquet garni (thyme, bay leaf, parsley)

Cut the lamb shoulder into large cubes.

Heat the olive oil in a large, heavy-based casserole and add the cubes of lamb. When they are lightly browned, discard the oil and replace the casserole over a medium heat. Add the basil, cover and leave to stew gently for about 30 minutes, stirring from time to time. If necessary, add a little water.

Peel the garlic and onions. Shell the peas and broad beans and top and tail the French beans. Peel the carrots and turnips and cut into chunks. Scrape the asparagus stems and wash the artichokes.

Add all the vegetables and the Veal Stock to the casserole, season with salt and pepper and add the bouquet garni. Cover and leave to cook for a further 25 minutes over a very low heat.

When you are ready to serve, transfer all the meat and vegetables to a large, deep serving dish and keep hot.

Place the casserole with the cooking liquor back over a high heat and reduce it by half, then pour over the meat and vegetables. Be careful not to break the asparagus, which are very delicate.

Serve immediately.

My Tip

I sometimes like to serve this lamb navarin just with potatoes from the island of Noirmoutier, off the French Atlantic coast, simply strewn with small pieces of salted butter from Guérande, in Brittany.

Small stuffed Provençal-style vegetables

PREPARATION TIME: 25 MINUTES / COOKING TIME: 40 MINUTES

Serves 4

**100 g (3½ oz) basmati rice · 1 red pepper
1 green pepper · 1 yellow pepper · 4 ripe but firm tomatoes
4 small round courgettes · 4 onions · 1 garlic clove
5 tbsp olive oil · 200 g (7 oz) lean minced beef
herbs (chives, tarragon, chervil, flat-leaf parsley)
salt and freshly ground pepper · 1 egg yolk
30 g (1 oz) freshly grated Parmesan cheese**

Cook the rice in plenty of salted water for about 8 minutes then drain. While the rice is cooking, wash the vegetables and pat dry on kitchen paper. Remove the stalks from the peppers, cut in half lengthways and remove the seeds and white parts from inside. Cut lids from the tomatoes about one-third of the way down and hollow them out with a spoon, setting the pulp and lids aside. Cut lids from the courgettes, one-third of the way down, and spoon out the pulp, leaving a little adhering to the sides. Peel the onions and cut off the tops, also one-third of the way down, and hollow them out with a spoon.

Roughly chop all the pulp taken from the tomatoes, courgettes and onions. Peel and chop the garlic and add to the chopped vegetables. Heat 2 tbsp olive oil in a large, heavy-based casserole and fry the vegetables. When they have reduced down, add the meat and herbs. Season with salt and pepper and stir well, cover and cook for about 3 minutes then mix with the cooked rice, the egg yolk and Parmesan cheese and use this mixture to stuff all the small vegetables. Place all the reserved lids on the vegetables.

Preheat the oven to 200°C/400°F/gas mark 6. Pour the rest of the olive oil into a large baking tin and arrange the stuffed vegetables in it. Cook in the preheated oven for about 40 minutes, making sure that they do not burn.

When the vegetables are ready, remove them from the oven and serve immediately on a bed of mixed wild salad herbs or rocket.

Pot-au-feu with four types of meat

PREPARATION TIME: 50 MINUTES / COOKING TIME: 1 HOUR 40 MINUTES

Serves 4

**1 calf's tongue • 500 g (1 lb 2 oz) spare ribs • 500 g (1 lb 2 oz) veal fillet
1 litre (1¾ pints) Chicken Stock (see page 66) or Veal Stock (see page 79)
1 bouquet garni (thyme, bay leaf, parsley)
1 onion, peeled and studded with a clove • 1 chicken
To serve 500 g (1 lb 2 oz) broccoli • 500 g (1 lb 2 oz) small asparagus
4 regular or 8 cherry tomatoes • 1 yellow pepper • 8 purple artichokes
2 courgettes • 2 potatoes**

Place the calf's tongue, the spare ribs and the fillet of veal into a large saucepan, add enough water to cover and bring to the boil. Leave to blanch for 30 minutes, skimming the surface regularly.

Lift out the meats with a slotted spoon and wash thoroughly under cold running water. Carefully skin the tongue and remove all the horny parts.

Place the Chicken or Veal Stock (or you could use a stock cube), the bouquet garni and onion in a large saucepan and bring to the boil.

Discard the blanching water and return the meats to the pan. Add the hot stock and return to a slow boil. Leave to simmer for 1 hour then add the chicken, adding more water if necessary. Cover and leave to cook for 45 minutes.

About 15 minutes before the meats have finished cooking, prepare the vegetables: clean, peel, wash and dry the broccoli and asparagus.

Wash the tomatoes and pepper and blanch them in boiling water, leaving the tomatoes for 10 seconds and the pepper for 1 minute to make them easy to peel. Wash the artichokes, courgettes and potatoes; cut the artichokes in half, the courgette into short lengths and quarter the potatoes.

Separately, cook the broccoli for 10 minutes and the asparagus for 15 minutes in a little of the stock taken from the casserole. Cut the pepper into strips and add it, together with the other vegetables, to the casserole and cook for the last 15 minutes of the cooking time.

When the meats are ready, cut the tongue and fillet of veal into slices then cut the chicken and spare ribs into pieces, and place in a deep serving dish. Drain the vegetables well and arrange them in colourful groups around the meat: white asparagus, green broccoli, red tomatoes and yellow peppers. Pour a few ladles of the stock over the dish and serve straightaway.

FISH AND SHELLFISH

Buying fish is a good reason for going to the market early in the morning and watching the stalls fill up with fish freshly caught from the Breton fishing boats. There is a wonderful display of crayfish, lobster and sardines, of halibut and bass, of cod – my favourite fish –, whiting (try my recipe for Whiting Colbert) and, in the right season, scallops and oysters, not forgetting the many varieties of mussels, cockles and clams. The smell of salt and the invigorating sea air never fail to bring an exuberant atmosphere to fish markets.

Fresh tuna with chanterelles

PREPARATION TIME: 25 MINUTES / COOKING TIME: 20 MINUTES

Serves 4

a piece of tuna cut from the thickest part • 100 ml (3½ fl oz) olive oil
1 bunch of small onions, preferably just pulled
4 garlic cloves, preferably just pulled
600 g (1¼ lb) small, very fresh chanterelles
fine sea salt and freshly ground black pepper
1 bunch of chervil or tarragon

Wash the tuna under cold running water, pat dry on kitchen paper and cut it into slices, dipping the slices into olive oil as they are cut.

Peel the onions and garlic. Cut the onions into thin rings and the garlic into small strips. Wash the chanterelles and cut off the hard ends of the stalks. If they are small, keep them whole, otherwise cut them into pieces.

Heat the olive oil used for dipping the tuna in a large frying pan. Add the slices of fish and seal on both sides. They should be well browned on the outside but still tender inside.

In another frying pan, fry the onions and chanterelles in a small amount of oil. When they are lightly browned add the garlic.

Five minutes before serving, add the tuna to the onions and chanterelles and sauté over a high heat.

To serve, place the slices of tuna on warmed plates and surround them with the onions and chanterelles. Sprinkle with a little fine sea salt and some sprigs of chervil or tarragon.

Season with a few twists of the pepper mill and serve immediately.

My Tip

Instead of tuna I also like to use swordfish, that delicious fish known in France as the 'veal of the sea' because its flavour and texture are somewhat reminiscent of veal.

Tuna steak with artichokes, flavoured with curry

PREPARATION TIME: 30 MINUTES / COOKING TIME: 40 MINUTES

Serves 4

2 onions • 1 garlic clove • 3 small peppers
2 tomatoes • 2 tbsp olive oil • salt and freshly ground black pepper
a pinch of curry powder • 4 slices of light tuna
8 small purple artichokes • 2 tbsp flat-leaf parsley

Peel and roughly chop the onions and garlic. Wash the peppers and remove the seeds then cut the pepper into strips. Blanch the tomatoes in boiling water, peel, cut them in half then remove the seeds and mash the pulp.

Heat the olive oil in a large, heavy-based casserole and brown all the prepared vegetables. Stir and season with salt, pepper and the curry powder, then cover and leave to cook for about 15 minutes.

Add the tuna slices, re-cover and braise for about 10 minutes.

Discard the artichoke stalks and cut the artichokes in half. Normally they contain little or no choke but discard any you find. Drop the artichokes into a pan of boiling salted water and blanch for 5 minutes. Drain and dry them on kitchen paper then add to the casserole with the parsley, finely chopped. Cover again and leave to cook for a further 10 minutes.

Place the tuna steaks on warmed plates surrounded by the artichokes, then spoon over the cooked vegetables and serve.

My Tip

The little purple artichokes are my favourites, especially eaten raw with a drizzle of oil, a little fine sea salt, freshly ground black pepper and sun-dried tomatoes.

Smoked haddock with 'boulangère' potatoes

PREPARATION TIME: 30 MINUTES / COOKING TIME: 30 MINUTES

Serves 4

**50 g (2 oz) butter • 800 g (1¾ lb) smoked haddock • 1 litre (1¾ pints) milk
salt and freshly ground black pepper • 1 lemon • ½ bunch of flat-leaf parsley**
For the 'boulangère' potatoes **1 glass of Chicken Stock (see page 66) • 1 glass of white wine
1 kg (2¼ lb) small firm waxy potatoes, such as Charlotte or Ratte • 1 bunch of small onions,
preferably just pulled • 30 g (1 oz) lightly salted butter • salt and freshly ground black pepper**

Preheat the oven to 220°C/425°F/gas mark 7. Grease a large baking dish with the butter.

To prepare the 'boulangère' potatoes: heat the Chicken Stock and wine in a large saucepan. Wash and peel the potatoes and place them in the boiling liquid, adding enough water to cover. Cook for 10 minutes then drain the potatoes in a colander and leave to cool. As soon as the potatoes are cool, slice them into round slices. Peel the onions and cut them into rings. Heat the lightly salted butter in a frying pan and brown the onions. Add the sliced potatoes and let them brown lightly on both sides then arrange them in the greased baking dish. Bake in the hot oven for 20 minutes, adding a little extra water if necessary to keep the potatoes soft.

Clean and trim the haddock then rinse under cold running water and cut into four pieces. Place the haddock pieces in a large saucepan and cover with the milk. Season with pepper and bring to a slow boil. Cook for about 15 minutes, skimming the surface from time to time.

When the haddock is cooked, lift it out of the pan with a slotted spoon and place the pieces on warmed plates.

Make some clarified butter by melting the butter in a small saucepan and removing the foam that rises to the surface with a small spoon or some kitchen paper.

Coat the pieces of fish with the clarified butter, moisten with a few drops of lemon juice and sprinkle over the washed and finely chopped parsley. Serve immediately, together with the 'boulangère' potatoes.

My Tip

I sometimes serve this haddock with a Hollandaise sauce made with 8 egg yolks whisked with 250 g (9 oz) of butter in a double saucepan. I add some salt and pepper and a pinch of cayenne pepper.

Salt cod with aïoli sauce

PREPARATION TIME: 1 HOUR / COOKING TIME: 30 MINUTES
SOAKING TIME: 24 HOURS / PREPARE A DAY AHEAD

Serves 4

**1 kg (2¼ lb) salt cod fillets • 200 ml (7 fl oz) dry white wine
1 tbsp olive oil • 1 bouquet garni • 4 small onions • 24 whelks
24 winkles • 4 eggs • 4 tomatoes • 8 potatoes • 4 carrots
4 courgettes • 4 small purple artichokes • 1 head of celery
8 small squid • 1 tbsp olive oil**
For the aïoli sauce **4 garlic cloves • 2 egg yolks
salt and freshly ground black pepper • 100 ml (3½ fl oz) olive oil
juice of ½ lemon**

Soak the salt cod fillets in a large bowl of cold water for 24 hours to remove the excess salt, changing the water from time to time.

The next day, pour the wine and oil into a large saucepan, add the bouquet garni and onions and bring to the boil. Add the whelks and winkles and cook for about 30 minutes then drain in a colander, reserving the liquor, and set aside until required.

Poach the cod in the same liquor for 8–10 minutes. Meanwhile, hard-boil the eggs for 9 minutes. Wash the tomatoes and cut them into pieces.

Peel the vegetables, cut into large pieces and cook them in a steamer for 10 minutes.

To prepare the squid: clean and remove the transparent central spine then cut them into rings.

Heat the olive oil in a frying pan and brown the squid rings. Leave to drain on kitchen paper.

To prepare the aïoli: peel the garlic and remove the small shoots at the centre then pound the garlic to a smooth paste in a mortar. Add the egg yolks, salt and pepper and stir vigorously while slowly drizzling in the olive oil, as you would to make mayonnaise. Add a few drops of lemon juice and set aside in a cool place until required.

To serve, cut the cod into good-sized pieces and place them in the centre of a large, deep serving dish. Surround them with the vegetables and the eggs, quartered, the whelks, winkles and squid, and all the garnishes. Serve the aïoli sauce separately in a sauceboat.

Back steaks of fresh cod

PREPARATION TIME: 10 MINUTES / COOKING TIME: 10 MINUTES
STANDING TIME: 1 HOUR

Serves 4

2 good-sized pieces of cod, cut from the centre back
2 tbsp coarse salt · 3 tbsp extra virgin olive oil · fine sea salt
freshly ground black pepper · ½ bunch of basil · 1 lemon

Wash the cod, leaving the skin on. Place the coarse sea salt in a shallow dish, add the cod and leave to stand for 1 hour. Rinse the cod under cold running water and pat dry on kitchen paper.

Heat 1 tbsp olive oil in a large frying pan. Cut each piece of cod into two steaks and brown them for 5 minutes on each side.

When the steaks are lightly browned, arrange them on a warmed plate and sprinkle with the fine sea salt and pepper.

Cut the lemon into wedges or slices. Drizzle the remaining olive oil over the cod steaks and garnish with the lemon wedges or slices and basil sprigs. Serve immediately.

Brandade of salt cod

PREPARATION TIME: 20 MINUTES / COOKING TIME: 15 MINUTES
SOAKING TIME: 24 HOURS / PREPARE THE DAY BEFORE

Serves 4

**800 g (1¾ lb) salt cod fillets • 250 ml (9 fl oz) milk • 250 ml (9 fl oz) extra virgin olive oil
2 garlic cloves • salt and freshly ground black pepper • nutmeg • 1 lemon, preferably organic
To serve 1 stale baguette • 2 garlic cloves • 2 tbsp olive oil • 12 black olives**

Soak the salt cod fillets in a large bowl of cold water for 24 hours to remove the excess salt, changing the water from time to time. It must be completely desalinated.

When you come to prepare the salt cod, drain in a colander then place in a large saucepan, cover with cold water and bring slowly to the boil. Leave to simmer for 15 minutes then drain again. Remove the skin and bones and keep the flesh hot.

Heat the milk in a saucepan and the olive oil in another. Break up the cod into flakes and place them in a mortar, add the peeled garlic and pound the mixture until fairly thick.

Transfer the cod mixture to a large saucepan, place over a low heat and stir constantly, adding the milk then the oil alternately, a little at a time, making sure it does not boil.

When it has reached the desired consistency, remove the pan from the heat, stop stirring and add no more liquid. Taste and adjust the seasoning, grating in a little nutmeg. Mix well.

Cut the baguette into small round slices, rub with garlic and fry in olive oil. Stone the olives.

Serve very hot with the olives and fried round slices of baguette. Brandade of salt cod may also be served cold on a rocket salad.

My Tip

If, despite your best efforts, the consistency is not stiff enough, mix in a potato, baked in its skin then mashed with a fork; this will thicken the mixture. Try to buy good-quality lemons, preferably organic unwaxed ones. I like to purchase lemons from Menton, a city in the Alpes Maritimes, which is famous for its lemon production and lemon festival.

Skate wings with capers and lemon

PREPARATION TIME: 15 MINUTES / COOKING TIME: 25 MINUTES

Serves 4

4 skate wings
100 g (3½ oz) lightly salted butter
50 g (2 oz) capers
salt and freshly ground black pepper
2 lemons

Wash the skate wings and pat dry on kitchen paper then cook in a steamer for about 20 minutes. Skin the fish and remove all the bones.

Make clarified butter by melting the butter in a saucepan and skimming off the foam that rises to the surface.

Arrange the skate wings on warmed plates and pour the clarified butter over them. Add the capers and season with salt and pepper. Cut the lemon into wedges and use to garnish the skate.

Serve the skate with 'English style' potatoes (see my tip below).

My Tip

To prepare potatoes 'English style', peel some potatoes and cook in a pan of boiling salted water for 10 minutes. Drain and serve with a little melted butter and some chopped parsley. This recipe is dedicated to my daughter Julie.

Sardines marinated in olive oil

PREPARATION TIME: 15 MINUTES / MARINATING TIME: 1 HOUR

Serves 4

**20 fat fresh sardines • 100 ml (3½ fl oz) extra-virgin olive oil
juice of 3 limes • fine sea salt and freshly ground black pepper • 4 onions**

Clean the sardines and carefully scale them. Gut and wash them then pat dry on kitchen paper. Remove the backbones.

Pour the olive oil and the juice from the limes into a deep dish. Season with salt and pepper then cover the sardines with clingfilm and leave to marinate for about 1 hour, turning them once or twice.

To serve: roughly drain the marinated sardines and arrange them in a star-shape on individual plates. Peel the onions and cut into rings and place them on top of the sardines. Sprinkle with fine sea salt and serve immediately.

They are especially nice served with toasted slices of bread drizzled with a little of the marinade and sprinkled with dried oregano.

Whiting Colbert

PREPARATION TIME: 15 MINUTES / COOKING TIME: 15 MINUTES

Serves 4

4 fresh whiting • 3 heaped tbsp plain flour • 2 eggs • salt and freshly ground black pepper
3 tbsp breadcrumbs • oil for deep-frying • ½ bunch of flat-leaf parsley • 2 lemons

Clean the whiting and pat dry on kitchen paper. Give the fish a quick jerk on the tail to dislodge the backbone, then remove it and pull out the small bones with the aid of tweezers. Set the fish aside.

Spread the flour out in a shallow dish, break the eggs into a second shallow dish, season with salt and pepper and beat lightly, and put the breadcrumbs in a third.

Heat the oil in a deep-fat fryer to 180°C/350°F.

Quickly coat the whiting with the flour, one by one, then dip them in the egg and finally roll them in the breadcrumbs. When they are well coated, carefully place them in the hot oil and leave to cook for about 15 minutes.

As soon as the fish are cooked, lift out with a slotted spoon and arrange them in a warmed serving dish. Surround them with the lemons, cut in half and, before serving, scatter with chopped washed and dried flat-leaf parsley.

Soles meunière

PREPARATION TIME: 20 MINUTES / COOKING TIME: 15–20 MINUTES

Serves 4

4 soles, skinned and trimmed by the fishmonger
salt and freshly ground black pepper
plain flour · 50 g (2 oz) lightly salted butter
2 lemons · ½ bunch of flat-leaf parsley

Wash the soles in cold water then pat dry on kitchen paper. Make small cuts in the flesh at regular intervals to help the fish cook evenly, and season with salt and pepper. Spread the flour out on a plate and use to lightly flour the fish, shaking off any excess.

In two frying pans large enough to contain all the fish, heat half the butter. When it begins to foam, add the fish and cook for 5 minutes on each side. Check that they are cooked with the point of a knife; if the part nearest the bone is slightly pink then they are perfectly cooked. If not, leave for a few moments longer.

Discard the butter from the pans and keep the fish hot. Meanwhile, in a small saucepan, melt the rest of the butter and pass it through a conical or fine sieve to clarify it.

When ready to serve, pour the clarified butter over the soles, surround them with lemon slices and season with pepper to taste. Snip the flat-leaf parsley, previously washed and dried, over the fish and serve immediately.

My Tip

This simple, basic recipe can also be applied to salmon, hake, trout or even lemon soles.

Red mullet with saffron

PREPARATION TIME: 20 MINUTES / COOKING TIME: 40 MINUTES

Serves 4

**500 g (1 lb 2 oz) firm, waxy potatoes, such as Charlotte or Ratte • pinch of powdered saffron
16 small red mullet preferably caught in rocky waters • 3 tbsp olive oil
50 g (2 oz) butter • fine sea salt • freshly ground black pepper • a few whole chive lengths**

Cook the potatoes in a saucepan of saffron-flavoured boiling water for 10 minutes.

To prepare the mullet: cut off the heads and tails and slit them down the front. Open them out and remove the backbone. Take the creamy substance from the mullet and place in a frying pan with the olive oil.

When the potatoes are cooked, drain and leave to cool. Once cool, cut into round slices and arrange in a serving dish. Heat the pan containing the creamy parts of the mullet over a very low heat, add the mullet and cook for 3 minutes on each side, adding the butter, cut into small pieces. Season with salt and pepper and shake gently so as not to break the mullet, which are very fragile.

To serve, lay the mullet on the sliced potatoes, pour over the butter, sprinkle with sea salt and black pepper and garnish with a few whole chive lengths.

Monkfish à l'américaine

PREPARATION TIME: 30 MINUTES / COOKING TIME: 25 MINUTES

Serves 4

**1 tbsp plain flour • 800 g (1¾ lb) monkfish, cut into lengths • 2 tbsp groundnut oil
2 tbsp brandy • 2 shallots • 500 g (1 lb 2 oz) fresh tomatoes
salt and freshly ground black pepper • 100 ml (3½ fl oz) dry white wine • 30 g (1 oz) butter**

Spread the flour out on a plate and use to flour the monkfish pieces, tapping lightly to shake off any excess.

Heat the groundnut oil in a large, heavy-based casserole and brown the pieces of monkfish on all sides then pour in the brandy and set alight.

Peel the shallots, cut into large pieces and add to the casserole. Cover and cook over a very low heat. Blanch the tomatoes in boiling water for 1 minute then peel, cut in half and remove the seeds. Chop the flesh roughly and add to the casserole. Season with salt and pepper and add the wine. Cover and leave to simmer for 20 minutes.

When the monkfish is just cooked, lift out with a slotted spoon and arrange them in a serving dish. Pass the sauce through a fine sieve and whisk in the butter until incorporated. Serve the sauce either in a sauceboat or poured over the fish.

Baby squid with garlic and parsley

PREPARATION TIME: 20 MINUTES / COOKING TIME: 15 MINUTES

Serves 4

800 g (1¾ lb) fresh baby squid • 4 garlic cloves, preferably just pulled
1 bunch of flat-leaf parsley • 50 g (2 oz) butter • salt and freshly ground black pepper

Clean the squid carefully and pull off the fine skin from the sacs then pat dry on kitchen paper.

Peel and finely chop the garlic. Wash, dry and finely chop the parsley.

Melt half the butter in a large frying pan and brown the squid for 5 minutes, stirring frequently, until they just begin to colour.

Drain the squid and discard the butter in the pan. Return the squid to the pan, add the chopped garlic and cook for a further 5 minutes. Add the rest of the butter and half the chopped parsley and stir well. When the squid are just cooked – when they are still tender – serve them right away, piping hot.

Sprinkle over the rest of the washed and dried parsley to serve.

Baby squid sautéed Luzienne style

PREPARATION TIME: 30 MINUTES / COOKING TIME: 30 MINUTES

Serves 4

2 onions • 5 garlic cloves • 1 green pepper • 1 red pepper
2 tomatoes • 5 tbsp olive oil • 800 g (1¾ lb) fresh baby squid
salt and freshly ground black pepper • a pinch of Espelette pepper or paprika

Peel and chop the onions and garlic. Cut the peppers in half, remove the seeds and cut the peppers into strips. Roughly chop the tomatoes into small cubes.

Heat 2 tbsp olive oil in a large frying pan and brown the onions and garlic. Add the peppers then the tomatoes. Cover and leave to simmer for 15 minutes.

Clean the squid, pull off the fine skin from the sacs then pat dry on kitchen paper.

Heat the rest of the oil in a separate large frying pan and sauté the squid. Add the onions, garlic, peppers and tomatoes to the pan then add salt, pepper and the Espelette pepper or paprika. Stir, cover and leave to cook for a further 15 minutes.

Fried baby squid

PREPARATION TIME: 30 MINUTES / COOKING TIME: 15 MINUTES

Serves 4

800 g (1¾ lb) baby squid • 30 g (1 oz) plain flour • oil for deep-frying • 2 lemons
½ bunch of flat-leaf parsley • 1 bowl of mayonnaise

Carefully clean the squid, wash them under cold running water, pull off the fine skin from the sacs and pat dry on kitchen paper. Carefully cut the squid into rings.

Place the flour in a large, deep dish and use to coat the squid rings, shaking off any excess. Lay the floured squid rings on kitchen paper.

Heat the oil in a deep-fat fryer until very hot then carefully drop the squid rings into the hot oil and deep-fry for 7–8 minutes. When the squid rings float to the surface and are golden brown lift them out with a slotted spoon and drain on kitchen paper. Keep hot until all the squid rings are cooked.

Cut the lemons into wedges. Wash and dry the parsley and roughly chop. Place the squid rings, the lemon wedges, the parsley and mayonnaise in serving dishes then take to the table and let everyone help themselves.

Stuffed squid

PREPARATION TIME: 20 MINUTES / COOKING TIME: 45 MINUTES

Serves 4

**2 red peppers • 200 g (7 oz) ceps • 500 g (1 lb 2 oz) small squid • 1 onion • 2 garlic cloves
2 tbsp olive oil • 1 small glass of fish soup • ½ slightly stale baguette • 100 g (3½ oz) butter
2 eggs • 50 g (2 oz) grated Parmesan cheese • 1 small chilli • salt and freshly ground black pepper**

Wash the peppers and dice. Wash the ceps, discard the stalks and roughly chop. Wash the squid and remove the central spine. Chop two squid finely. Sweat the onion and garlic, peeled and chopped, in 1 tbsp olive oil until soft then add the peppers, ceps and chopped squid. Stir, add the fish soup and simmer gently for 20 minutes.

Cut the baguette into croûtons, brown in the remaining oil then cool. Preheat the oven to 240°C/475°F/ gas mark 9. Take an ovenproof dish large enough to contain all the squid and grease with the butter. Mix the prepared pepper, cep and squid mixture with the croûtons, eggs, Parmesan cheese, chopped chilli and salt and pepper. Stuff the squid sacs with the mixture and secure the openings with cocktail sticks.

Arrange the squid in the greased dish and cook in the preheated oven for 20 minutes, adding a little water to the dish if necessary.

Moules marinière

Serves 4

3 l (5¼ pt) fresh rope-grown mussels
8 shallots • 1 bunch of parsley • 50 g (2 oz) butter
1 bouquet garni (thyme, parsley, bay leaf)
200 ml (7 fl oz) dry white wine
salt and freshly ground black pepper

Scrape the mussels and remove any beards that are still attached to them. Discard any with broken shells or any that refuse to close when tapped. Wash the mussels thoroughly in cold water and drain in a colander.

Peel and finely chop the shallots. Wash the parsley and chop half roughly. Separate the rest into leaves for the garnish.

Melt the butter in a large saucepan. Add the mussels, bouquet garni, shallots, white wine and half the parsley. Cover and cook over a high heat, shaking the pan occasionally until the mussels open.

As soon as the mussels have opened, lift out with a slotted spoon and place in a large, deep serving dish. Discard any mussels that remain closed. Discard the bouquet garni then reduce the cooking liquor by cooking over a high heat for 5 minutes. Season with salt and pepper, then pour the liquor over the mussels and garnish with the reserved parsley leaves.

My Tip

This simple moules marinière dish can be varied by adding thick crème fraîche or by serving them with a poulette sauce. This is made with crème fraîche beaten with egg yolks and seasoned with salt, freshly ground black pepper and lemon juice, then heated gently over simmering water in a double saucepan.

Grilled langoustines

PREPARATION TIME: 15 MINUTES / COOKING TIME: 10–15 MINUTES

Serves 4

20 large langoustines, preferably from Brittany
fine sea salt · freshly ground black pepper
2 tbsp olive oil · 30 g (1 oz) butter · ½ lemon
1 bowl of herbs (flat-leaf parsley, coriander, chives, tarragon)

Wash the langoustines under cold running water, pat dry with kitchen paper and cut in half lengthways. Season the cut sides with salt and pepper.

Brush some olive oil over a cast-iron griddle pan and heat until very hot. Sear the langoustines on the cut side then turn them over and cook the other side until the shells turn pale pink. Keep them hot while you prepare the butter to serve with them.

Melt the butter in a small sauccpan and remove the foam that rises to the surface with a small spoon. Squeeze the lemon and add the juice to the clarified butter, together with the herbs, washed and chopped, and mix well.

Leave the herb and lemon butter to heat gently before pouring it over the langoustines just before serving. Sprinkle with sea salt and plenty of pepper.

Serve immediately.

My Tip

For a change from this simple griddled langoustines recipe you could flambé them with 2 tbsp whisky or Cognac (after stage 2 of the recipe), then prepare the clarified butter – as in stage 3 – with a little added crème fraîche, some tomato purée and lemon juice, and pour this sauce over the langoustines.

Lobsters 'à la nage'

PREPARATION TIME: 30 MINUTES / COOKING TIME: 45 MINUTES

Serves 4

**2 carrots • 1 leek, white part only • 1 celery stick
1 garlic clove • 1 onion, peeled and studded with 2 cloves
1 bouquet garni (thyme, parsley, bay leaf)
salt and freshly ground black pepper
cayenne pepper • 1 glass of good white wine
4 lobsters, preferably from Brittany, weighing about 500 g (1 lb 2 oz) each
80 g (3¼ oz) lightly salted butter • ½ bunch of chervil**

Make a well-flavoured stock with the carrots, peeled and cut into round slices, the leek, washed and chopped, the celery de-stringed and roughly chopped, the garlic, peeled, the onion studded with cloves and the bouquet garni. Season with plenty of salt, pepper and a pinch of cayenne, add the wine and some water. Bring to the boil and leave the stock to simmer for about 30 minutes.

Bring the stock to a rolling boil, drop in the lobsters and cook for a good 10 minutes. As a guide, a 500 g (1 lb 2 oz) lobster needs to cook for 8–10 minutes.

Drain in a colander then break off the claws and cut the bodies in half lengthways.

Strain the stock through a conical or fine sieve. Place three ladles of the stock in a saucepan and reduce over a high heat then, while it is still hot, whisk in the cold butter and pour some of it over the half-lobsters. Pour the rest into a warmed sauceboat, break the shell of the claws and serve on deep, warmed plates. Garnish the half-lobsters with chervil sprigs and serve with the sauce.

My Tip

This recipe for lobster 'à la nage' could become a lobster 'pot-au-feu' if you strained the stock through a conical or fine sieve, added some crème fraîche and reduced it over a high heat then returned all the vegetables and the pieces of lobster back to the mixture.

Lobster à l'armoricaine

PREPARATION TIME: 1 HOUR / COOKING TIME: 30 MINUTES

Serves 4

200 g (7 oz) small vine-ripened tomatoes · 4 shallots
1 garlic clove · 4 small live lobsters, preferably from Brittany
1 tbsp groundnut oil · 1 tbsp brandy · 250 ml (9 fl oz) dry white Muscadet-type wine
1 bouquet garni (thyme, parsley, bay leaf) · salt and freshly ground black pepper
cayenne pepper · 50 g (2 oz) butter

Blanch the tomatoes in boiling water for 1 minute then drain, peel, cut in half and remove the seeds. Mash the pulp. Peel and finely slice the shallots and garlic.

To prepare the lobsters: make one quick cut with a large, heavy knife, splitting them in half lengthways. Remove the head and break the shell of the claws, cut the bodies into pieces, using the shell segments as a guide. Take out the stomach sac from the head, spoon the coral and the creamy parts into a small bowl and set aside.

Heat the groundnut oil in a large sauté pan and sauté all the lobster pieces over a very high heat until they turn bright red. Soak up the oil from the pan with kitchen paper, pour in the brandy and quickly flambé them.

Reduce the heat and add the chopped garlic and shallot. Cook until they are transparent then add the wine, tomatoes, bouquet garni, season with salt,

pepper and a pinch of cayenne and cook for about 10 minutes.

When the lobsters are cooked, lift them out with a slotted spoon and keep them hot. Reserve the cooking liquor.

Reduce the cooking liquor in a saucepan over a high heat and add the reserved coral and creamy parts of the head.

After about 10 minutes the sauce will be well reduced. Strain it through a conical or fine sieve, pressing firmly to extract all the juices. Pour the sauce back into the saucepan and heat over a high heat. Add the butter, cut into little pieces.

When the sauce is ready, pour it into a warmed sauceboat and serve with the lobster pieces. Alternatively, reheat the lobster pieces and sauce together in a large sauté pan.

Freshwater crayfish 'à la nage'

PREPARATION TIME: 15 MINUTES / COOKING TIME: 30 MINUTES

Serves 4

**1 kg (2¼ lb) freshly caught crayfish · 1 carrot · 1 onion · 1 litre (1¾ pints) water
salt and freshly ground black pepper · 1 bouquet garni (thyme, parsley, bay leaf)
1 bunch of flat-leaf parsley · 20 g (¾ oz) crème fraîche · 1 small can truffle juice (optional)**

Wash the crayfish quickly under cold running water then pat dry with kitchen paper.

Peel and chop the carrot and onion into rings.

Bring the water to the boil in a saucepan. Add 15 g (½ oz) salt, a little pepper, the vegetables and the bouquet garni and leave to simmer for about 15 minutes, skimming the surface regularly.

Drop the crayfish in and cook for 10 minutes. When the crayfish are cooked, drain in a colander but keep a little of the cooking liquor and add the parsley, chopped, to it.

Take the crayfish out of their shells, place them back into the reserved cooking liquor and reheat gently. Serve with the cooking liquor or with a little crème fraîche and, on festive occasions, a little can of truffle juice.

Scallops with artichokes

PREPARATION TIME: 20 MINUTES / COOKING TIME: 20 MINUTES

Serves 4

**12 purple artichokes • salt • juice of ½ lemon • 12 scallops • 70 ml (4½ tbsp) olive oil
1 small can truffle shavings • 50 g (2 oz) butter**

To cook the artichokes, bring a saucepan of water seasoned with salt and lemon juice to the boil. Add the artichokes and cook for about 10 minutes. Drain in a colander and squeeze out all the water.

Open the scallops and carefully clean them, removing the black thread and coral.

Heat the olive oil in a large frying pan and brown the scallops for 3 minutes on each side.

Drain the liquid from the can of truffle shavings into a small saucepan and heat gently then whisk in the butter to form an emulsion.

Arrange the scallops on warmed individual plates. Halve or quarter the artichokes and place them around the scallops. Add the truffle shavings to the emulsified butter, mix well and coat both scallops and artichokes with this truffle sauce. Serve this dish straight away.

113

MEAT AND POULTRY

The quality of a piece of meat depends on the skill of the butcher.
A good butcher knows everything about his animals; how to cut
them up and how to distinguish the subtle differences in flavour
of the various parts of the carcass. He also attaches vital importance
to where it came from. Whether you are buying a leg of lamb,
a beef rib, calves' liver, kidneys or other delicious offal, or indeed
a farm-raised chicken, a duck or a guinea fowl, it is essential to
check that the meat is perfectly fresh, was raised in the traditional
manner and is free of all additives.

Veal flank with caramelized carrots and small onions

PREPARATION TIME: 20 MINUTES / COOKING TIME: 1 HOUR 30 MINUTES

Serves 4

**3 tbsp olive oil • 1 kg (2¼ lb) veal flank, sliced • 2 tomatoes
100 g (3½ oz) fatty streaky bacon • 1 glass of white wine
2 glasses of Chicken Stock (see page 66) • 1 bouquet garni (thyme, parsley, bay leaf)
2 bunches of baby carrots • 1 bunch of small onions, preferably just pulled
30 g (1 oz) butter • salt and freshly ground black pepper • a pinch of sugar
powdered dried thyme or lavender**

Heat the olive oil in a large sauté pan and brown the veal slices on all sides.

Blanch the tomatoes in boiling water for 1 minute then peel and cut them in half, remove the seeds and cut the pulp into large pieces. Cut the bacon into lardons.

When the veal is well browned on both sides, discard the oil and add the tomatoes, bacon lardons, wine, 1 glass of Chicken Stock and the bouquet garni and leave to cook over a high heat.

Preheat the oven to 200°C/400°F/gas mark 6.
Peel the carrots and onions and leave them whole.

Place the onions in a sauté pan, cover and cook slowly in the oven for about 1½ hours.

Meanwhile, cook the carrots in the remaining Chicken Stock with the butter and a pinch of salt. When they are just tender, strain in a colander, return the cooking liquor to the pan, add the sugar and reduce to a thick, syrupy consistency over a high heat. Return the carrots to the pan and leave them to caramelize in the cooking juices.

To serve, remove the veal slices from the pan, drain off any excess liquid and lay them on warmed plates, surrounded by the caramelized carrots and the baked onions. Dust lightly with the powdered thyme or lavender and serve immediately.

Blanquette of veal cooked the old-fashioned way

PREPARATION TIME: 30 MINUTES / COOKING TIME: 1 HOUR 10 MINUTES

Serves 4

**1 kg (2¼ lb) breast or flank of veal, or a mixture of the two
2 onions • 2 carrots • 1 bouquet garni (thyme, parsley, bay leaf)
salt and freshly ground black pepper
For the Creole rice 100 g (3½ oz) basmati rice
500 ml (16 fl oz) Chicken Stock (see page 66)
or – better still – clear Veal Stock (see page 79)
For the sauce 40 g (1½ oz) butter • 20 g (¾ oz) cornflour
2 tbsp thick crème fraîche • 1 egg yolk • juice of ½ lemon
button mushrooms or field mushrooms or some of each
a knob of butter**

Cut the meat into large pieces, place in a large saucepan of cold water and bring to the boil. When it begins to bubble, cover and leave for about 10 minutes, skimming the surface frequently with a slotted spoon.

Drain the meat in a colander, discard the water, then return the meat to the pan. Add the onions and carrots, peeled and roughly chopped, and the bouquet garni. Cover with fresh cold water, season with salt and pepper and boil for 50 minutes. When the meat is cooked, keep hot while you finish the rest of the dish.

To make the sauce: slowly melt 30 g (1 oz) of butter in a small saucepan. Stir in the cornflour and leave to cook for a few minutes without browning. Gradually add some of the broth from the meat, strained through a conical or fine sieve, and stir to

make a fairly thick sauce then remove from the heat. In a bowl, mix the crème fraîche and egg yolk together. Stir in a little of the hot broth and pour this mixture into the prepared sauce, whisking constantly to ensure a smooth consistency. Add the lemon juice, taste and adjust the seasoning then set aside.

To prepare the Creole rice: wash the rice under cold running water, place in a saucepan with the Chicken or Veal Stock and leave to cook for about 15 minutes. Meanwhile, peel and chop the mushrooms and sauté them in a frying pan with the rest of the butter.

To serve, place the meat in the centre of a warmed serving dish, surround it with the rice, cover with the mushrooms and coat with the hot sauce.

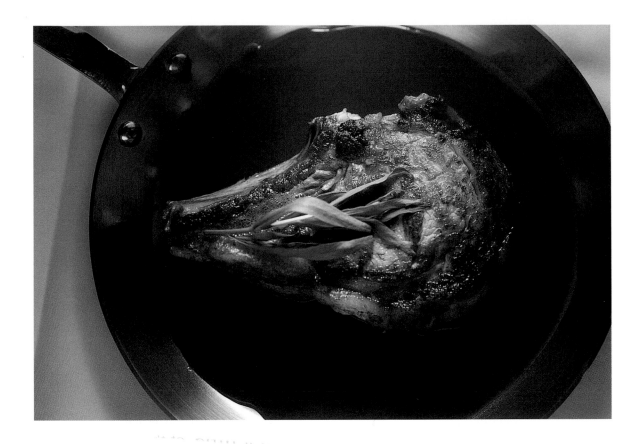

Veal cutlets with tarragon

PREPARATION TIME: 10 MINUTES / COOKING TIME: 20 MINUTES

Serves 4

30 g (1 oz) butter · 1 tbsp oil · 4 veal cutlets
1 good bunch of tarragon · 2 shallots
salt and freshly ground black pepper
100 g (3½ oz) crème fraîche (optional)

Heat 20 g (¾ oz) butter with the oil in a large frying pan. Brown the veal cutlets on both sides for about 6 minutes.

Wash the tarragon, strip off the leaves, set half aside and chop the rest. Peel and chop the shallots and sweat them in the remaining butter in a saucepan. When they are slightly transparent, add the chopped tarragon, season with salt and pepper and mix well. If you are using crème fraîche in this recipe, add this to the pan and heat gently.

When the cutlets are evenly browned on both sides, place them on warmed serving plates, coat them with the tarragon sauce and scatter with whole tarragon leaves.

Serve with ratatouille.

119

Roast knuckle of milk-fed veal with vinegar

PREPARATION TIME: 1 HOUR / COOKING TIME: 4 HOURS 30 MINUTES

Serves 4

**1 knuckle of veal • salt and freshly ground black pepper
1 carrot • 1 onion • 1 celery stick • fine sea salt**
For the veal stock **1 kg (2¼ lb) veal bones • 100 g (3½ oz) carrots
100 g (3½ oz) onions • 100 g (3½ oz) white part of leek
100 g (3½ oz) celery • 1 bouquet garni (thyme, parsley, bay leaf)
salt and freshly ground black pepper • 50 ml (2 fl oz) aged wine vinegar
4 garlic cloves • 2 bay leaves • 1 kg (2¼ lb) firm, waxy potatoes, such as Charlotte or Ratte**

To prepare the veal stock: roughly chop the veal bones and place them in a large stockpot, cover with cold water and bring to the boil. Skim regularly, adding more water as necessary. Remove any fat that rises to the surface then add the peeled carrots, onions, leeks, celery and the bouquet garni. Leave to cook for about 3 hours, skimming regularly. At the end of the cooking time, leave the stock to cool then strain through a conical or fine sieve. You can use it immediately or bottle it for future use.

To prepare the veal knuckle: preheat the oven to 190°C/375°F/gas mark 5. Season the meat with salt and pepper. Peel the carrot and onion, de-string the celery and roughly chop them all.

Place the knuckle in a large, cast-iron casserole. Add the vegetables and 2 glasses of veal stock and cover with a lid. Place the casserole in the preheated oven and leave to cook for 1 hour, turning the knuckle so that it cooks evenly.

Towards the end of this cooking time, increase the oven temperature to 200°C/400°F/gas mark 6. Transfer the cooking liquor to a saucepan together with the wine vinegar and reduce it by half over a high heat. Return the reduced liquor to the casserole with the knuckle, add the whole garlic cloves and bay leaves and return to the oven for a further 30 minutes.

Serve the knuckle and garlic cloves with whole steamed potatoes sprinkled with fine sea salt.

Calf's head with gribiche sauce

PREPARATION TIME: 1 HOUR / COOKING TIME: 1 HOUR 30 MINUTES

Serves 4

**1 calf's head, boned, with the tongue and the brain • salt
2 tbsp white vinegar • 2 carrots • 2 onions • 2 cloves • 2 leeks
50 g (2 oz) cornflour • 100 ml (3½ fl oz) dry white wine
coarse salt • 1 tbsp black peppercorns • 1 tbsp pink peppercorns
1 bouquet garni (thyme, parsley, bay leaf) • 8 potatoes • 2 juniper berries
50 g (2 oz) plain flour • 40 g (1½ oz) butter
For the gribiche sauce 2 eggs • 1 tsp strong mustard • 200 ml (7 fl oz) olive oil
2 chopped gherkins • 2 tbsp chopped capers
2 tbsp finely chopped herbs (chervil, parsley, tarragon)
salt and freshly ground black pepper**

Wash the head thoroughly and soak the brain in iced water for 15 minutes.

Place the calf's head and tongue in a large saucepan, cover with cold water, add salt and the vinegar and bring to the boil.

Peel and finely chop the carrots. Peel the onions and stud them with the cloves. Wash the leeks, cut into lengths and tie them into little bunches.

Drain the calf's head and wash it in cold water. Trim it carefully, removing any fat and cut it into pieces. Place the head in a large saucepan with the tongue, cover with cold water and boil for a further 1 hour. Add the cornflour, white wine, carrots and onions, leeks, coarse salt, the black and pink peppercorns, the juniper berries, the bouquet garni and potatoes. Leave to simmer for 30 minutes.

To prepare the gribiche sauce: Hard-boil the eggs for 9 minutes. Cool them under cold running water, then shell them and leave to cool completely.

Cut the cooled eggs in half and mash the yolks with the mustard and olive oil, then add the whites, finely chopped. Add all the remaining ingredients and the herbs then season with salt and pepper. Taste the sauce to adjust the seasoning if necessary.

Drain the calf's head in a colander, skin the tongue and cut it into slices. Take the brain out of the water, dry and cut it into 4 pieces. Spread the flour out on a plate and use to flour the pieces of brain, shaking off any excess. Heat the butter in a frying pan and fry the brain.

Arrange the pieces of head, the slices of tongue and the brain in a large serving dish. Serve the potatoes and vegetables separately. Serve the gribiche sauce in a sauceboat.

Calf's liver Lyonnaise style

PREPARATION TIME: 15 MINUTES / COOKING TIME: 15 MINUTES

Serves 4

**20 g (¾ oz) plain flour • 4 slices of calf's liver, about 125 g (4 oz) each
salt and freshly ground black pepper • 50 g (2 oz) butter • 4 onions • a dash of wine vinegar
2 tbsp white wine or Chicken Stock (see page 66) • 1 bunch of flat-leaf parsley**

Lightly flour the slices of liver, shaking off any excess. Season with salt and pepper.

Melt 30 g (1 oz) butter in a large frying pan and fry the slices of liver for 4 minutes on each side if you like it pink, or 6 minutes if you prefer it cooked for slightly longer.

Peel and finely slice the onions and sweat them in 20 g (¾ oz) butter. Add some of the cooking juices from the liver, drizzle over the vinegar and leave to cook until soft.

When the onions are cooked, transfer the liver to a large, warmed serving dish and place the onions on top of them. Swill the pan with the wine or Chicken Stock, then reduce the liquor and pour it over the liver. Snip some parsley over just before serving and garnish with sprigs of parsley.

Grenadins of veal with broad beans and chanterelles

PREPARATION TIME: 15 MINUTES / COOKING TIME: 30 MINUTES

Serves 4

500 g (1 lb 2 oz) small chanterelles · 1 bunch of tarragon
600 g (1¼ lb) fresh broad beans · 30 g (1 oz) butter
4 thick round slices cut from the veal fillet
salt and freshly ground black pepper

Wash the chanterelles and trim the stalks. If they are small, leave them whole, otherwise cut into pieces. Wash the tarragon and strip off the leaves. Pod the broad beans.

Heat the butter in a large frying pan. Season the veal steaks with salt and pepper and brown them over a high heat, turning them several times to absorb the butter. Cover the pan and leave to cook for about 10 minutes. They should remain moist and pink in the centre.

Meanwhile, steam the broad beans or boil in a saucepan of salted water.

When the grenadins are the colour of hazelnuts, take them out and keep them hot while you cook the chanterelles in the same pan. Sauté the chanterelles for 5 minutes then add the well drained broad beans, mix in the tarragon and cook for a further 5–10 minutes.

At the end of the cooking time, return the veal to the pan, check the seasoning and serve immediately, piping hot.

My Tip

Grenadins are to veal what tournedos are to beef,
that is to say, round slices cut from the thickest
part of the fillet. They are expensive to buy,
but their texture and flavour are
both incomparable.

Steak tartare made with tail-end of fillet

PREPARATION TIME: 15 MINUTES / NO COOKING REQUIRED

Serves 4

600 g (1¼ lb) tail-end of beef fillet
salt and freshly ground black pepper • 8 gherkins
4 small white onions • 4 eggs • 1 tbsp capers
1 tsp mustard • 1 tbsp each chervil, tarragon and flat-leaf parsley
extra virgin olive oil • Worcestershire sauce
Tabasco sauce • ketchup

Cut the meat into small cubes then chop it finely with a knife. Season with salt and pepper and divide it into 4 equal portions, flatten with dampened hands then cover with clingfilm and leave in the refrigerator until required.

Cut the gherkins into tiny cubes. Peel and chop the small white onions.

Separate the eggs and leave the yolks in the shell.

Make a well in the centre of each portion of chopped meat and add the egg yolks. Place the gherkins, onions, capers, mustard and the herbs in separate small bowls.

To serve, place the 'tartares' in the centre of individual plates and take them to the table together with the prepared small bowls and bottles of extra virgin olive oil, Worcestershire sauce, Tabasco and ketchup. The diners can then prepare their own steak tartare in the way they like it.

My Tip

I particularly like this recipe because everyone can season the tartare according to their own taste.

Beef carpaccio

PREPARATION TIME: 10 MINUTES / NO COOKING REQUIRED

Serves 4

600 g (1¼ lb) best quality beef fillet
100 ml (3½ fl oz) extra virgin olive oil, preferably one from Tuscany
freshly ground black pepper • 1 tsp fine sea salt
8 fresh capers • basil leaves

Place the meat in the freezer for 15 minutes to make it firm and easier to slice.

Brush 4 serving plates with olive oil. Slice the meat as finely as possible (preferably with an electric slicer) and arrange the slices on the prepared plates. Drizzle some olive oil over them, season with pepper and sea salt and sprinkle with capers. Garnish with basil leaves.

Serve the carpaccio with extra olive oil in a bottle on the table and perhaps a rocket salad and some shavings of Parmesan cheese.

Entrecôte bordelaise

PREPARATION TIME: 20 MINUTES / COOKING TIME: 30 MINUTES

Serves 4

4 thick entrecôte steaks · 1 tbsp oil
10 g (¼ oz) butter · ½ bunch of flat-leaf parsley
For the bordelaise sauce **4 shallots · 100 ml (3½ fl oz) red wine**
1 bouquet garni (thyme, parsley, bay leaf)
salt and freshly ground black pepper
100 ml (3½ fl oz) Veal Stock (see page 79)
50 g (2 oz) butter

To prepare the bordelaise sauce: peel and finely chop the shallots, place them in a small saucepan with the red wine, bouquet garni and pepper and bring to the boil. Reduce by half then add the Veal Stock and reduce again. Add the butter, cut into small pieces, and whisk to emulsify the sauce then keep hot while you cook the steaks.

Heat a cast-iron griddle pan and oil it lightly. Place the steaks on the griddle pan and cook for about 4 minutes on each side, turning the steaks through 90-degrees to mark them with a lattice pattern.

When the meat is cooked to your satisfaction, transfer it to warmed serving plates, coat with the bordelaise sauce and sprinkle with parsley.

My Tip

It is even better with beef marrow, but has a higher fat content. If you are not worried about cholesterol, tie two marrow bones in a piece of muslin and cook for 40 minutes in boiling salted water. Drain, scrape out the marrow and cut it into rounds and top the steaks with them. Sprinkle with fine sea salt.

Flank of sirloin with shallots

PREPARATION TIME: 10 MINUTES / COOKING TIME: 10–15 MINUTES

Serves 4

2 tbsp good red wine · 50 g (2 oz) butter
12 shallots · salt and freshly ground black pepper
600 g (1¼ lb) sirloin flank, cut into steaks (this is a French
cut of beef with coarse, long filaments)
100 ml (3½ fl oz) Chicken Stock (see page 66) · 1 tbsp oil

Heat the Chicken Stock with the red wine in a saucepan and leave to reduce by half, about 15 minutes. Whisk in 30 g (1 oz) butter, cut into small pieces, and keep hot until required.

Peel and finely chop the shallots and sweat them in a frying pan in the rest of the butter until they are transparent. Season with salt and pepper and leave to cook until lightly caramelized. When they are the colour of hazelnuts, mix the shallots into the red wine sauce and reheat gently.

Heat a cast-iron griddle pan and oil it lightly. Place the steaks on to the pan and grill for 3 minutes on each side. They should still be pink in the centre. Once they are cooked to your liking, season with salt and pepper and transfer to warmed serving plates.

Coat the steaks with the red wine and shallot sauce and serve immediately with a Buttered Potato Purée (see page 166) or some salsify (see page 159).

My Tip

If you can't get sirloin flank steaks, you could use 'hampe' or 'onglet' – more French cuts with the same coarse, long-fibre texture and an incomparable flavour – or sirloin steaks.

Strung fillet of beef

PREPARATION TIME: 30 MINUTES / COOKING TIME: 10 MINUTES

Serves 4

4 carrots • 4 leeks • 4 small turnips • 8 white onions
1 head of fennel • 1 celery stick • 2 litres (3½ pints) water
1 chicken stock cube • 1 bouquet garni (thyme, parsley, bay leaf)
1 kg (2¼ lb) beef fillet • sea salt • freshly ground black pepper
gherkins • mustard

Peel the carrots, leeks, turnips, onions and fennel, de-string the celery and cut them all into large pieces or if small leave them whole.

Bring the water to the boil in a large saucepan. Add the stock cube, bouquet garni, carrots, leeks, turnips, onions, celery and fennel and leave to cook for 30 minutes.

Cut the meat into 4 round slices 4 cm (1½ in) thick, bind them with kitchen string and place them on a wooden spoon so they can be plunged into the stock and held just under the liquid.

When the stock has returned to the boil, plunge the meat into the stock and leave to cook for about 7–8 minutes, according to how well-cooked you like it. For this recipe I recommend rapid cooking so that the blood is trapped inside and the meat stays nice and red and remains tender.

Lift the meat out of the cooking liquor and remove the strings, then place them on soup plates. Take out the vegetables with a slotted spoon and arrange them around the meat. Season with salt and pepper. Serve the mustard and gherkins separately according to individual preference.

My Tip

To give extra flavour to the stock, add one or two marrow bones and a piece of fatty streaky bacon at the start of cooking.

Beef bourguignon

PREPARATION TIME: 30 MINUTES / COOKING TIME: 1 HOUR 45 MINUTES
MARINATING TIME: 12 HOURS / PREPARE THE DAY BEFORE

Serves 4

1 kg (2¼ lb) braising beef, such as chuck steak, neck, etc.
2 tbsp sunflower oil • 50 g (2 oz) butter • 1 tbsp plain flour
salt and freshly ground black pepper • 100 g (3½ oz) button mushrooms
100 g (3½ oz) pearl onions • 100 g (3½ oz) piece of lean bacon
100 g (3½ oz) croûtons (optional)
For the marinade **2 shallots • 2 carrots • 1 bottle of good red Burgundy wine**
2 tbsp sunflower oil • 1 good-sized onion, peeled and studded with 2 cloves
1 bouquet garni (thyme, parsley, bay leaf) • 1 tsp crushed peppercorns
To serve **8 firm, waxy potatoes, such as Charlotte or Ratte**
30 g (1 oz) melted butter • 1 bunch of flat-leaf parsley

Prepare the marinade the day before: peel and finely chop the shallots and carrots. Cut the meat into large cubes and place them in a terrine with the wine, sunflower oil, onion, carrots, shallots, bouquet garni and the crushed pepper. Stir, then cover and leave to marinate for at least 12 hours.

The next day, prepare the meat: drain it from the marinade and pat dry on kitchen paper. Strain the marinade and set aside.

Heat the oil and 30 g (1 oz) butter in a large, cast-iron casserole and brown the meat on all sides then remove the meat and discard the cooking fat. Heat 20 g (¾ oz) of butter in the casserole and add the meat and any juices that have run from it then sprinkle in the flour and stir well. Bring the marinade to the boil and pour over the flour mixture, stirring constantly. Season with salt and pepper, cover and leave to simmer for 1½ hours. At the end of the cooking time, taste and adjust the seasoning if necessary.

Wash and roughly chop the mushrooms. Peel the onions and finely dice the bacon.

Heat the diced bacon in a frying pan. Add the onions and mushrooms and leave to cook gently for 15 minutes. After the meat has been cooking for 1 hour 15 minutes, add the bacon mixture to the casserole and cook for a further 10 minutes.

Pierce the meat with a fork to check if it is tender. If not, leave for a few more minutes.

Cook the potatoes 'English style': that is, peeled and boiled in salted water for 15 minutes then drained and coated in melted butter and scattered with parsley.

Lift out the meat with a slotted spoon and place in the centre of a deep serving dish surrounded by the potatoes. Ladle over the vegetables and bacon, sprinkle over the croûtons if using, and serve.

Beef in white wine

PREPARATION TIME: 1 HOUR / COOKING TIME: 4 HOURS 15 MINUTES
MARINATING TIME: 2 HOURS

Serves 4

**75 g (3 oz) fatty streaky bacon · 1 kg (2¼ lb) beef, such as rump or shoulder
60 ml (4 tbsp) brandy, preferably Cognac · 200 g (7 oz) streaky smoked bacon with rind
4 small carrots · 4 shallots · 2 garlic cloves · ½ calf's foot, cut into slices by your butcher
1 onion, peeled and studded with 2–3 cloves · 1 bouquet garni (thyme, parsley, bay leaf)
salt and freshly ground black pepper · freshly ground nutmeg
400 ml (14 fl oz) dry white wine · 500 ml (16 fl oz) Veal Stock (see page 79)
1 bunch of parsley**

Cut the fatty bacon into strips and briefly freeze. Using a sharp knife, make holes in the beef and insert the bacon strips into them. Place the meat in a bowl and pour over the brandy, then cover and leave to marinate in the refrigerator for about 2 hours, turning frequently.

Cut the rind from the streaky bacon and set aside. Finely dice the bacon, peel and slice the carrots and shallots. Peel and finely chop the garlic.

Brown the diced bacon in a large frying pan until crispy, without using additional fat. Remove the beef from the marinade, pat dry and add to the bacon with the calf's foot. Brown the meat well on all sides. Remove the pan from the heat and take out the contents from the pan.

Place the bacon rind at the base of the pan, then place the carrots on top. Return the diced bacon, beef and calf's foot to the pan, then add the shallots, garlic, onion studded with cloves and the bouquet garni. Season with salt, pepper and a pinch of nutmeg. Pour over the wine and Veal Stock, then cover and simmer gently for 4 hours. Do not lift the lid during cooking.

Wash the parsley and shake dry, remove the leaves and chop finely. Before serving, remove the onion studded with cloves and the bouquet garni from the sauce, then take the beef and slices of calf's foot out the sauce. Cut the beef into slices and cut the meat from the calf's foot slices. Arrange both kinds of meat with the vegetables on a warmed serving dish and sprinkle with the parsley. Skim any fat from the sauce using a slotted spoon, then either pour over the meat or serve separately. Serve with fresh baguette or potatoes boiled in their skins.

Ox cheek with carrots and calf's feet

PREPARATION TIME: 1 HOUR / COOKING TIME: 3 HOURS

Serves 4

200 g (7 oz) butter · 1 kg (2¼ lb) ox cheek
salt and freshly ground black pepper · 100 ml (3½ fl oz) water
2 litres (3½ pints) full-bodied red wine · 2 calf's feet, split in half
1 bunch of onions, preferably just pulled · 1 kg (2¼ lb) carrots, preferably baby ones
40 g (1½ oz) plain dark chocolate

Preheat the oven to 150°C/300°C/gas mark 2. Melt 50 g (2 oz) of butter in a large, cast-iron casserole over a fairly high heat and fry the ox cheeks on all sides until lightly browned. Season with salt and pepper, add the water and a similar amount of red wine and stir with a wooden spoon to dissolve the residue clinging to the dish.

Add the calf's feet, split into halves, cover and cook in the preheated oven for 2–3 hours, checking occasionally to make sure that the meat does not dry out. Add more water and wine as necessary.

Peel and quarter the onions. Add the onions after 1½ hours of the cooking time and continue cooking.

Peel and trim the carrots. Leave whole if they are small baby ones, otherwise cut into little batons.

Melt 50 g (2 oz) of butter in a saucepan and stew the carrots gently for about 10 minutes with a little salt and pepper and a few tbsp of water.

When the carrots are lightly browned on all sides, drain and add them to the casserole and leave to cook for a further 20 minutes.

Take the calf's feet out of the casserole and carefully bone them. Remove the meat and cut into even slices.

When ready to serve, lift the carrots and onions out from the cooking liquor and arrange them in a warmed serving dish. Lay the slices of meat on top, surround them with the boned calf's feet and keep hot while you prepare the sauce.

Ladle the cooking liquor through a conical or fine sieve into a saucepan, pressing it well with a wooden spoon to squeeze out all the goodness then set it over a medium heat, add the chocolate, roughly chopped, and the rest of the butter, cut into small pieces. Whisk until it is well emulsified and a good dark colour. Pour some of the sauce over the ox cheeks.

Serve the ox cheeks with the remaining sauce in a sauceboat.

Pork fillet with mustard sauce

PREPARATION TIME: 30 MINUTES / COOKING TIME: 30 MINUTES

Serves 4

600 g (1¼ lb) pork fillet • 2 tbsp oil • 40 g (1½ oz) butter
salt and freshly ground black pepper
For the mustard sauce **2 shallots • 6 gherkins • ½ bunch of tarragon**
125 ml (4 fl oz) dry white wine • 125 g (4 oz) cream
2 tbsp wholegrain mustard • 30 g (1 oz) cold butter
salt and freshly ground black pepper

Wash the pork fillet, pat dry on kitchen paper and cut into slices about 3 cm (1¼ inch) thick. Using a meat tenderizer or the base of a frying pan pound the medallions flat between two layers of clingfilm.

Heat the oil and butter − if necessary in portion-sized batches − in a large frying pan. Cook the medallions for about 4 minutes on each side. Season with salt and pepper. Remove the medallions from the pan, reserving the cooking fat, and keep warm.

Meanwhile, to make the sauce: peel the shallots and dice finely. Dice the gherkins, wash the tarragon and shake dry, then pull the leaves from the stalk and chop finely.

Sweat the shallots in the cooking fat from the medallions until softened. Pour in the wine and leave to reduce slightly. Add the cream, stir in the mustard and leave to simmer for about 5 minutes over a low heat.

Cut the butter into small pieces and stir into the mustard sauce. Finally add the gherkins and the tarragon, then season with salt and pepper.

Arrange the medallions and the mustard sauce on warmed serving plates. Buttered Potato Purée (see page 166) is an ideal accompaniment to this dish.

My Tip

This mustard sauce is a classic recipe from the Burgundy region. In spring and summer I like to replace the gherkins with a bunch of mixed herbs.

Pork loin stuffed with herbs

PREPARATION TIME: 40 MINUTES / COOKING TIME 50 MINUTES

Serves 4

200 ml (7 fl oz) milk · 4 slices of baguette (one day old)
1 bunch each of parsley, chervil, tarragon and chives · 1 carrot
1 onion · 1 garlic clove · 200 g (7 oz) button mushrooms
sea salt and freshly ground black pepper
3 kg (6½ lb) boneless pork loin joint with rind · 2 tbsp butter
200 ml (7 fl oz) Veal Stock (see page 79)
a dash of brandy, preferably Cognac

Preheat the oven to 190°C/375°F/gas mark 5. To prepare the stuffing: heat the milk gently. Remove the crusts from the bread and place in the hot milk for a few minutes to soften. Wash the herbs and shake dry, then remove the leaves and chop finely. Snip the chives into small pieces. Peel the carrot, onion and garlic, and dice finely. Clean the mushrooms, dry on kitchen paper and cut into slices.

Remove the bread from the milk, squeeze out the excess milk with your hands and tear into pieces. Mix in a bowl with the prepared herbs, carrot, onion, garlic and mushrooms. Season with salt and pepper.

Place the pork loin on a chopping board, rind facing downwards, and place the stuffing in the centre. Bring the joint together and tie with kitchen string to secure. Score the rind with a sharp knife.

Melt the butter in a heavy-based casserole and brown the pork loin on all sides over a medium heat. Pour in the Veal Stock, then cover with a lid and cook in the oven for 30 minutes per 450 g (1 lb) plus 35 minutes, adding a little water, if necessary, until cooked. For a crispy finish, remove the lid 10–15 minutes before the end of the cooking time, sprinkle the rind with a little sea salt and cook until crispy.

Remove the meat from the casserole and keep hot. Place the casserole on the hob, pour in the brandy and simmer until the liquor is reduced. Carve the pork into slices and serve the sauce as an accompaniment.

Spare ribs with honey and spices

PREPARATION TIME: 20 MINUTES / COOKING TIME: 30 MINUTES
MARINATING TIME: 30 MINUTES

Serves 4

125 g (4 oz) honey · **60 ml (4 tbsp) soy sauce**
60 ml (4 tbsp) sherry vinegar · **20 g (¾ oz) grated fresh root ginger**
½ tsp potato flour · **salt and freshly ground black pepper**
1 kg (2¼ lb) pork spare ribs · **a pinch of ground cumin**
a pinch of ground cinnamon · **a pinch of icing sugar**
1 glass of Chicken Stock (see page 66)

Mix the honey, soy sauce, sherry vinegar, ginger and potato flour together in a large, deep dish. Season with salt and pepper.

Cut the spare ribs into slices and add them to the marinade and leave to marinate for 30 minutes. Turn them several times so that the skin absorbs all the flavours. Sprinkle over the ground cumin, cinnamon and icing sugar then turn the spare ribs again in the marinade.

Lightly drain the spare ribs, reserving the marinade, and brown them in a large sauté pan for 5 minutes on each side, then add the Chicken Stock and 2 tbsp of the marinade and cook for a further 5 minutes.

Preheat the oven to 240°C/475°F/gas mark 9. Coat the base of a large ovenproof dish with the rest of the marinade and lay the spare ribs on it. Cook in the hot oven for 20 minutes, basting them with their cooking juices and turning regularly.

When the spare ribs are cooked, arrange them on warmed serving plates.

Heat the rest of the cooking liquor in a saucepan and reduce by half. Strain it through a conical or fine sieve and gently reheat it.

To serve, coat the ribs with the sauce and serve immediately, together with some Créole rice (see page 118) or prepared as a pilau.

My Tip

Créole rice (see page 118) is cooked in Chicken Stock, whereas pilau is first fried in a little oil with chopped small onions, then moistened with boiling water.

Pork chops charcutière style

PREPARATION TIME: 20 MINUTES / COOKING TIME: 30 MINUTES

Serves 4

**1 glass of Veal Stock (see page 79) • 2 onions
3 shallots • 4 pork loin chops • 20 g (¾ oz) butter
100 ml (3½ fl oz) white wine • 50 ml (2 fl oz) aged wine vinegar
salt and freshly ground black pepper • 6 gherkins
4 flat-leaf parsley sprigs • 1 tsp mustard • 1 tbsp sunflower oil**

To prepare the sauce: heat the Veal Stock gently in a saucepan. Peel and finely chop the onions and the shallots.

Heat half the butter in a small saucepan and fry the onions and shallots until lightly browned. Add the white wine and vinegar and reduce by two thirds.

When the sauce is reduced, add the Veal Stock and reduce again. Season with salt and pepper and leave on a very low heat.

Finely chop the gherkins and the parsley and add them to the sauce. Stir in the mustard, cover and turn off the heat.

Heat the remaining butter and the oil in a large frying pan and fry the pork chops for 6 minutes on each side.

When they are nicely browned transfer the pork chops to warmed serving plates and coat with the reduced sauce.

These pork chops could be served with Buttered Potato Purée (see page 166) or a Gratin Dauphinois (see page 168).

My Tip

I sometimes put tarragon and capers in my sauce.

Slow-cooked milk-fed lamb with spices and dried fruit

PREPARATION TIME: 20 MINUTES / COOKING TIME: 2 HOURS

Serves 4

**1 kg (2¼ lb) neck of lamb · 500 ml (16 fl oz) olive oil
a pinch of ground ginger · a pinch of powdered saffron
a pinch of cayenne pepper · a drop of vanilla extract
2 bunches of fresh thyme · 1 head of garlic, preferably just pulled
salt and crushed peppercorns · 100 ml (3½ fl oz) Chicken Stock (see page 66)
200 g (7 oz) dried apricots · 200 g (7 oz) prunes · a pinch of ground cinnamon
a pinch of ground cumin · 200 g (7 oz) couscous · 30 g (1 oz) butter**

Cut the neck of lamb into good-sized pieces and brown in the olive oil in a large, cast-iron casserole. Add a little water and leave to simmer slowly for 1 hour.

When the pieces of lamb are just tender, remove from the casserole.

Preheat the oven to 190°C/375°F/gas mark 5. Place all the aromatic ingredients – the ginger, saffron, cayenne, vanilla, thyme, garlic, salt and crushed peppercorns in the casserole. Mix well and replace the meat, together with some of its cooking liquor. Add enough Chicken Stock just to cover the meat, cover and place in the oven. Leave to simmer for 2 hours.

At the end of the cooking time, remove the casserole from the oven, pour some of the cooking liquor from it into a saucepan and reduce over a high heat. Add the apricots and prunes and leave them to swell in this stock. Sprinkle the ground cinnamon and cumin over and cook slowly for a further 10 minutes.

To prepare the couscous: take three ladles of the hot cooking liquor from the lamb and pour it over the couscous in a bowl. Leave to swell for about 10 minutes then place the couscous in a couscous cooker or steamer and steam for 15 minutes.

To serve: transfer the couscous to a serving dish and top with a little salted butter. Arrange the lamb, with the dried fruits, on the couscous and pour over the cooking juices.

Lamb curry

PREPARATION TIME: 30 MINUTES / COOKING TIME: 1 HOUR
MARINATING TIME: 1 HOUR

Serves 4

1 tbsp coriander seeds • 1 tbsp cumin seeds
1 tsp cardamom seeds • 1 tsp cinnamon • 2 cloves
½ tsp black peppercorns • ½ tsp red chilli powder
1 tsp turmeric • 200 ml (7 fl oz) red wine vinegar
a piece of fresh root ginger • 1 kg (2¼ lb) lamb shoulder
2 bay leaves • 3 garlic cloves • 1 tsp mustard seeds

Dry fry the coriander and cumin seeds in a frying pan then transfer them to a food processor with all the other spices and process to a fine powder. Add the chilli and turmeric and 1 tsp wine vinegar and mix well. Finely grate the ginger and add to the mixture. Place the paste in a shallow dish.

Cut the meat into large cubes. Place the meat into the prepared paste, lay the bay leaves on top and cover with the rest of the vinegar. Leave to marinate for 1 hour, if possible, covered with clingfilm. Stir the meat occasionally, and re-cover each time.

Preheat the oven to 180°C/350°F/gas mark 4.

Peel and chop the garlic and fry in a large, cast-iron casserole. Add the mustard seeds then the meat and marinade, season lightly with salt, bring to the boil then cover and cook in the hot oven for at least 1 hour.

At the end of the cooking time, check the meat: it should be moist and tender and some liquid should remain. Add a little hot water if necessary.

When the lamb is ready, serve the curry with Créole rice (see page 118) or plain boiled potatoes.

My Tip

To save time I suggest you prepare the ground spices in advance and store them in an air-tight jar then just add the vinegar and ginger.

'Half-wild' duckling with salt and pepper

PREPARATION TIME: 20 MINUTES / COOKING TIME: 1 HOUR

Serves 4

1 half-wild duckling, such as Barbary, bought ready-trussed
fine salt and freshly ground black pepper
1 bunch of thyme • 3 bay leaves
50 g (2 oz) butter • 4 shallots • 2 garlic cloves

Season the duckling with salt and pepper. Crumble half of the thyme and 1 bay leaf then roll the bird in this herb mixture, coating it on all sides.

Melt half of the butter in a large, cast-iron casserole and lightly brown the duckling on all sides.

Peel the shallots and garlic, leave whole and place them in the casserole. Add the remaining bay leaf and thyme. Cover and leave to cook slowly over a low heat for 45 minutes.

At the end of the cooking time, turn the bird over, re-cover and leave to cook for a further 15 minutes.

Melt the rest of the butter in a saucepan, skimming off the foam that forms on the surface. When the duck is cooked, remove from the casserole and pour the clarified butter over it.

Just before serving, cut the duck into generous pieces, arrange them in a deep serving dish and serve, garnished with the shallots and garlic.

Serve Caramelized Chicory (see page 152) as an accompaniment.

My Tip

If you can't find a Barbary duck, choose a mallard, or a cross-bred duck during the game season.

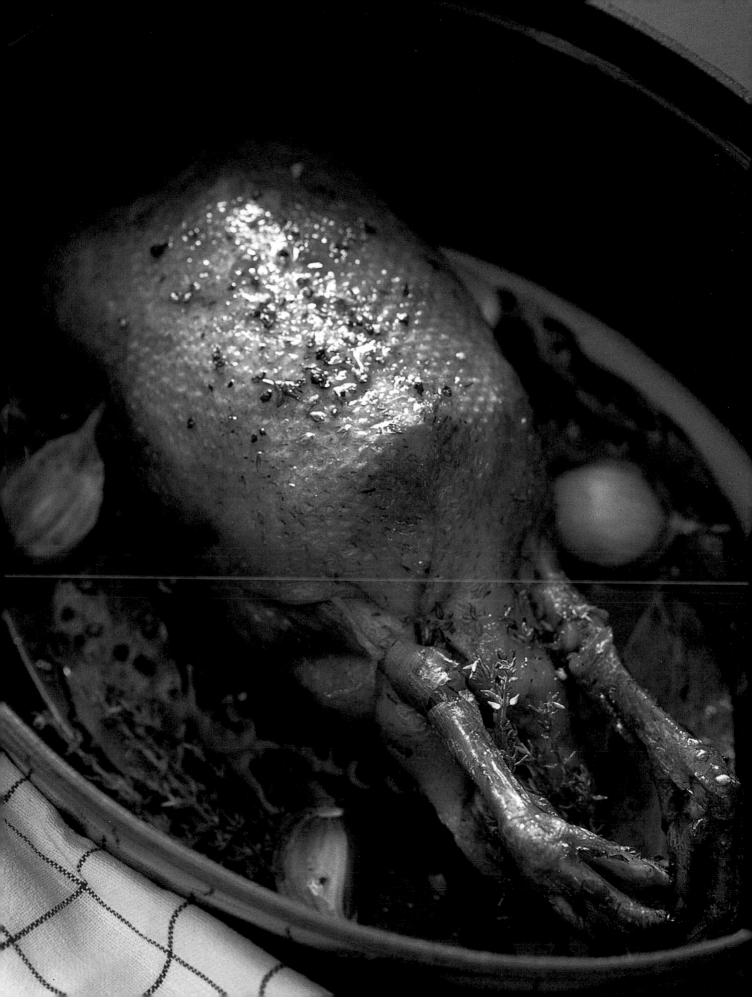

Small chicken with Diable sauce

PREPARATION TIME: 30 MINUTES / COOKING TIME: 45 MINUTES
MARINATING TIME: 3 HOURS

Serves 4

1 whole egg · 1 egg yolk · 1 tsp Dijon mustard
2 thyme sprigs · 100 ml (3½ fl oz) olive oil
salt and freshly ground black pepper
1 small chicken, preferably organic or from the Landes region
50 g (2 oz) butter · 100 g (3½ oz) breadcrumbs
For the Diable sauce 3 shallots · 1 bunch of tarragon
1 bunch of chervil · 100 ml (3½ fl oz) sherry vinegar
200 ml (7 fl oz) Chicken Stock (see page 66) or Veal Stock (see page 79)
100 g (3½ oz) butter · 1 tbsp wholegrain mustard
salt and freshly ground black pepper

Prepare a marinade by mixing the egg and egg yolk, Dijon mustard, thyme leaves and olive oil in a deep dish. Season with salt and pepper and whisk to form an emulsion.

Joint the chickens and place in the marinade, cover with clingfilm and leave to marinate in the refrigerator for 3 hours. Turn them from time to time to make sure they are well steeped in the marinade.

Preheat the oven to 220°C/425°F/gas mark 7. Grease a large, ovenproof dish with a little of the butter.

Place the breadcrumbs in a deep plate and roll the chicken joints in them, making sure they are well coated, then arrange them in the greased dish. Place a knob of butter on each piece and cook in the oven for 20–25 minutes.

Meanwhile, prepare the Diable sauce: peel the shallots and finely chop with the tarragon and chervil. Pour the sherry vinegar into a saucepan, add the herbs and shallots and cook until the vinegar has evaporated, then add the Chicken or Veal Stock and leave to reduce by half. Gradually add the butter, a small piece at a time, and whisk to form a smooth emulsion.

Strain the sauce through a conical or fine sieve, add the wholegrain mustard and season with salt and pepper, then pour into a warmed sauceboat, and keep hot.

Remove the chicken from the oven and arrange the pieces on warmed serving plates. Serve with the Diable sauce, offered separately in the sauceboat.

Small chicken cooked in *vin jaune* with morels

PREPARATION TIME: 25 MINUTES / COOKING TIME: 45 MINUTES

Serves 4

200 g (7 oz) fresh morels or 60 g (2¼ oz) dried morels
1 small chicken, preferably organic or from Bresse or Houdan
20 g (¾ oz) plain flour · 30 g (1 oz) butter · 2 tbsp groundnut oil
2 shallots · 2 glasses of *vin jaune* or *vin de paille* (see tip)
1 glass Chicken Stock (see page 66) · 50 g (2 oz) thick crème fraîche
salt and freshly ground black pepper

Wash the morels. If using dried morels, soak them in a bowl of warm water for about 2 hours at room temperature.

Cut the chicken into 6 pieces, quickly roll them in the flour, then shake off any excess.

Heat 10 g (¼ oz) butter and the oil in a large, cast-iron casserole, add the pieces of chicken and brown on all sides.

Peel and chop the shallots and add them to the casserole. Add the wine and boil to reduce, then add enough Chicken Stock just to cover the chicken pieces. Cook slowly over a medium heat.

Trim the ends of the morel stalks and wash them to eliminate any sand. If using dried ones, drain them in a colander and reserve the soaking water.

Heat the rest of the butter in a large sauté pan, add the morels and sauté for 10 minutes.

When the pieces of chicken are cooked, lift them out with a slotted spoon, place them on warmed serving plates and keep them hot.

Reheat the cooking juices together with the morel soaking liquid until hot then strain the sauce through a fine sieve and add the crème fraîche and salt and pepper. Mix well, pour over the pieces of chicken and surround them with the morels.

My Tip

If you have time, mix 30 g (1 oz) plain flour with 50 g (2 oz) softened butter until it forms a smooth paste, omit the crème fraîche and use the paste to thicken the sauce before serving. Vin jaune (yellow wine) *and* vin de paille *are famous wines from the Jura mountain region.*

Duck with turnips

PREPARATION TIME: 20 MINUTES / COOKING TIME: 1 HOUR

Serves 4

1 onion • 2 garlic cloves • 600 g (1¼ lb) small turnips • 20 g (¾ oz) butter
1 duck, preferably Barbary or Aylesbury, cut into pieces
100 g (3½ oz) fatty streaky bacon • 1 bouquet garni
½ bottle of good red wine • salt and freshly ground black pepper

Peel and finely chop the garlic and onion. Cut the bacon into lardons. Peel the turnips, leaving them whole if they are small, otherwise roughly chop into large pieces.

Melt the butter in a large, cast-iron casserole and fry the pieces of duck until they are nicely browned on all sides. Drain and discard the fat, leaving the pieces of duck in the casserole.

Add the garlic and onion, the bacon lardons, the turnips, the bouquet garni and the red wine. Season with salt and pepper and cook for 1 hour, uncovered, stirring occasionally.

When the duck is cooked to your taste, take out the pieces, arrange them in a large serving dish and serve immediately, together with the turnips, which should be lightly caramelized.

Fricassee of chicken with crayfish

PREPARATION TIME: 30 MINUTES / COOKING TIME: 40 MINUTES

Serves 4

**24 freshwater crayfish • 100 g (3½ oz) pearl onions
100 g (3½ oz) small button mushrooms • juice of ½ lemon
2 tbsp oil • 1 chicken, preferably organic or one from Bresse,
weighing about 2 kg (4½ lb), jointed • 30 g (1 oz) butter
1 glass of dry white wine • salt and freshly ground black pepper
20 g (¾ oz) crème fraîche**

Wash the crayfish and pull out the black intestinal thread, which would leave a bitter taste if left. If you are unable to buy crayfish, use langoustines instead and shell them before use.

Peel the onions and wash the mushrooms and roughly chop. Sprinkle the mushrooms with the lemon juice.

Heat the oil in a large, cast-iron casserole and fry the pieces of chicken. When they are lightly browned all over, discard the oil and add the butter. Leave this to melt then add the onions and mushrooms. Return the pieces of chicken to the casserole and moisten with the wine. Season with salt and pepper then cover and leave to cook for about 30 minutes.

After 20 minutes, remove the casserole from the heat, turn the chicken pieces over, add the crayfish and return the casserole to a medium heat.

When the chicken is cooked, arrange it in a warmed serving dish, surround it with the crayfish and mushrooms and keep hot.

Pour the cooking juices from the chicken into a saucepan and reduce over a high heat then strain through a conical or fine sieve.

Return the sauce to the pan and reheat gently. Stir in the crème fraîche and pour some of the sauce over the chicken until coated. Serve the remaining sauce separately in a well-warmed sauceboat.

Serve rice or fresh pasta with this dish.

My Tip

If you cannot buy crayfish you could use langoustines as an alternative.

Guinea fowl with cabbage

PREPARATION TIME: 30 MINUTES / COOKING TIME: 1 HOUR

Serves 4

1 guinea fowl weighing about 1 kg (2¼ lb)
salt and freshly ground black pepper • 2 tbsp oil
1 glass of Chicken Stock (see page 66)
For the stuffing **1 glass of milk • 2 slices of bread from a tin loaf**
1 egg • nutmeg • 1 bunch of tarragon
1 bunch of flat-leaf parsley • 1 bunch of chives
For the buttered cabbage **2 carrots • 2 onions**
2 garlic cloves • 1 nice round Savoy cabbage
100 g (3½ oz) butter • 1 small glass of white wine

Remove the liver and gizzard from the guinea fowl and set aside. Season the bird generously with salt and pepper.

To prepare the stuffing: warm the milk gently in a saucepan. Place the bread in the milk to soften then squeeze out the excess with your hands. Place the soaked bread in a large bowl, add the egg, a little grated nutmeg, half of the tarragon, parsley and chives, chopped, and mix well. Roughly chop the liver and gizzard, add to the bread mixture and mix well. Fill the bird with the stuffing, close the opening and tie the bird with kitchen string.

Heat the oil in a large, cast-iron casserole and brown the guinea fowl, turning frequently. Add the Chicken Stock and cook for about 30 minutes, turning the bird over occasionally and adding a little water if required.

To prepare the buttered cabbage: peel the carrots and cut into rings. Peel and chop the onions and garlic. Wash the cabbage and cut out the hard stem. Discard the outside leaves and finely shred

the heart then plunge it into a saucepan of boiling salted water for 1 minute or until just tender. Drain thoroughly.

Add the carrots, onions and garlic to the casserole with the guinea fowl and continue cooking.

Melt half the butter in a large frying pan. Add the shredded cabbage and stir until it has soaked up the butter, then add the wine and leave to cook, covered, for about 15 minutes.

When the guinea fowl is cooked, cut the bird into joints and slice the stuffing. Strain the cooking juices through a conical or fine sieve into a saucepan, reheat it and gradually whisk in the rest of the butter, a small piece at a time, to form an emulsion.

Lay the cabbage on a deep serving dish and arrange the pieces of guinea fowl and slices of stuffing on top. Pour the sauce over until the guinea fowl is coated and sprinkle with the rest of the chopped fresh herbs.

Rabbit with rosemary

PREPARATION TIME: 20 MINUTES / COOKING TIME: 1 HOUR 15 MINUTES

Serves 4

6 shallots · 4 pink garlic cloves · 4 rosemary sprigs
50 g (2 oz) butter · 1 good fat rabbit, cut into pieces
1 glass of dry white wine · 1 glass of water
salt and freshly ground black pepper

Peel the shallots and garlic, leaving them whole. Strip the leaves from the rosemary.

Melt the butter in a large, cast-iron casserole. Add the pieces of rabbit and leave them to brown on all sides. When they are coloured all over, add the wine and water. Season with salt and pepper, add the rosemary, the shallots and garlic, then cover and cook for 1 hour, turning the pieces once or twice during cooking.

Serve the rabbit straight from the casserole.

VEGETABLES AND SIDE DISHES

One can live perfectly well on a mixture of vegetables, accompanied by rice, pasta, lentils (or other dried pulses), as long as the diet contains proteins. Nothing is more delicious than vegetables in season: the astringent flavour of asparagus, the slightly bitter taste of spinach, the crunchiness of French beans or the mysterious, subtle flavours of edible mushrooms. I grew up with an extreme fondness for potatoes and later discovered pasta in all its shapes and sizes. Then rice came along to add an exotic touch to otherwise ordinary stews. The simplest of dishes can be transformed into a feast.

Caramelized chicory

PREPARATION TIME: 20 MINUTES / COOKING TIME: 45 MINUTES

Serves 4

1.25 kg (2¾ lb) chicory • 50 g (2 oz) butter
40 g (1½ oz) brown sugar
2 tbsp runny honey
fine sea salt and freshly ground black pepper

Wash the chicory and strip off any spoiled leaves. Using a sharp knife, cut out the bitter-flavoured conical base to a depth of about 1 cm (½ in). Pat dry on kitchen paper.

Bring a large saucepan of water to the boil. Add the chicory and cook for 5 minutes then drain and dry well on kitchen paper. Leave to cool.

Melt half the butter in a large sauté pan and brown the chicory, then add the sugar and let it form caramel, stirring with a wooden spoon to prevent the sugar from sticking to the sides of the pan.

Add a little water, and leave the chicory to absorb the colour, turning from time to time. Drizzle over the honey and stir until mixed. Season with a little sea salt and pepper, then steam over a low heat for about 30 minutes, turning the chicory halfway through the cooking time and adding a little water, if necessary. Add the rest of the butter then cover with a lid and continue steaming until it is golden brown and cooked.

Arrange the chicory heads in a warmed serving dish and season with sea salt and coarsely ground black pepper to taste.

My Tip

Chicory is one of my favourite vegetables – particularly when the rather bitter chicory heads are prepared with sugar and honey. Caramelized chicory is best served with scallops or a simple cooked ham.

Petits pois French style

PREPARATION TIME: 30 MINUTES / COOKING TIME: 20 MINUTES

Serves 4

**1 kg (2¼ lb) very small fresh garden peas · the heart of 1 lettuce
1 bunch small onions, preferably just pulled, or pearl onions
3 baby carrots · 50 g (2 oz) butter
1 bouquet garni (thyme, parsley, bay leaf)
salt and freshly ground black pepper · 1 sugar cube**

Shell the peas, wash the lettuce and shred it. Peel the onions and discard their green stalks. Wash the carrots, scrape them if necessary and cut into rings.

Melt half the butter in a large pan. Add the peas, bouquet garni, shredded lettuce, carrot rings and onions. Stir and add a little water then season with salt and pepper. Add the sugar cube, cover and cook over a low heat for about 20 minutes.

At the end of the cooking time the peas should be tender. Taste and leave to cook longer if they are still a little hard.

When the peas are ready, transfer to a large, warmed serving dish, add the rest of the butter, cut into small pieces, stir well and serve them alongside the dish of your choice.

My Tip

If you are not familiar with petits pois cooked Nantes style, here is the recipe: cook the peas with small cubes of tomato, a bunch of flat-leaf parsley and lamb's lettuce.

Asparagus with mustard sauce

PREPARATION TIME: 20 MINUTES / COOKING TIME: 20 MINUTES

Serves 4

1.5 kg (3¼ lb) white asparagus, preferably organic or from Chinon
For the mustard sauce **200 g (7 oz) thick crème fraîche**
2 tbsps olive oil · 1 tbsp Dijon or wholegrain mustard
salt and freshly ground black pepper · 1 bunch of chervil

Trim the ends of the asparagus and peel them carefully then cook in a steamer for 20 minutes.

Meanwhile, prepare the mustard sauce: beat the crème fraîche and olive oil together in a bowl. Add the mustard and salt and pepper and mix to a smooth, creamy consistency. Strip off the chervil leaves and add half of them to the mustard sauce. Mix well.

When the asparagus is ready, drain in a colander, wrap in kitchen paper and squeeze them gently to remove excess liquid, taking care not to break them.

If you prefer the asparagus cold, leave them to cool at room temperature, wrapped in the kitchen paper. Then lay in an asparagus or ordinary serving dish and leave in a cool place until required.

If you prefer the asparagus warm, when ready to serve, put the still-warm asparagus on serving plates, sprinkle it with the remaining chervil leaves and serve with the mustard sauce.

My Tip

The success of this simple recipe is heavily dependant on the quality of the asparagus; the asparagus grown in Chinon are particularly good.

Green asparagus with vierge sauce

PREPARATION TIME: 20 MINUTES / COOKING TIME: 20 MINUTES

Serves 4

2 good bunches of green asparagus
For the Vierge sauce **100 ml (3½ fl oz) extra virgin olive oil · juice of ½ lemon**
1 tsp fine sea salt · freshly ground black pepper
To garnish **star anise · a few tomatoes dried with garlic (optional)**

Trim the end of the asparagus but peel only if necessary. Cook it for 15 minutes in a steamer or in a metal sieve set over a saucepan of boiling water.

To prepare the vierge sauce: whisk the olive oil and lemon juice together to form an emulsion. Add a little of the salt and some freshly ground pepper.

When the asparagus is still a little firm, drain it on kitchen paper and leave to cool. If necessary, squeeze it very gently to remove any excess water.

To serve, arrange it in a long serving dish and pour the sauce over it.

Garnish with star anise and a few dried tomatoes with garlic, if you like.

Artichokes 'barigoule'

PREPARATION TIME: 30 MINUTES / COOKING TIME: 1 HOUR

Serves 4

12 purple artichokes • 2 carrots • 2 shallots • 20 g (¾ oz) butter
1 glass of white wine • 1 glass of Chicken Stock (see page 66) • 3 tbsp olive oil
1 bouquet garni (thyme, parsley, bay leaf) • sea salt and freshly ground black pepper
1 lemon • 8 black olives, stoned • 1 star anise • 1 bay leaf • peppercorns • lemon zest

Wash the artichokes and discard the stems and green outer leaves then cut them in half. To prepare the 'barigoule': peel the carrots and shallots and chop them finely.

Melt the butter in a large, cast-iron casserole and fry the chopped vegetables for 5 minutes. Pour in the wine, Chicken Stock and olive oil. Add the bouquet garni, season and cook for 10 minutes.

Add the artichokes, the lemon, sliced, the olives, star anise and bay leaf and cook for 20 minutes.

Drain the artichokes reserving the cooking liquor, olives, star anise and bay leaf. Pour the liquor into a saucepan, reduce over a high heat then pass through a sieve. Pour this sauce over the artichokes. Garnish with the olives, star anise, bay leaf, peppercorns and lemon zest.

Spinach with double cream

PREPARATION TIME: 10 MINUTES / COOKING TIME: 30 MINUTES

Serves 4

1.5 kg (3¼ lb) fresh spinach · 30 g (1 oz) butter
100 ml (3½ fl oz) double cream
(with 40 per cent fat, or use thick crème fraîche)
1 glass of Chicken Stock (see page 66)
salt and freshly ground black pepper · nutmeg (optional)

Wash the spinach thoroughly and remove any hard stalks. Drain and dry on kitchen paper.

Melt the butter in a large sauté pan and add the spinach leaves, stirring well with a wooden spoon. Cover with a lid and leave to cook over a very low heat for 20 minutes.

Meanwhile, warm the cream in a saucepan. Add the Chicken Stock and simmer slowly to reduce the cream by one third.

When the spinach is completely softened, drain and chop it roughly with a knife and pour the cream over it. Mix well, season with salt and pepper and leave to simmer over a very low heat. Taste and adjust the seasoning if necessary. Grate a little nutmeg over, if you like.

My Tip

This simple recipe is my favourite one for spinach because it retains its distinctive flavour but is made soft and creamy by the crème fraîche. The traditional accompaniments for spinach are eggs (Spinach Florentine) or red or white meat. Spinach is also excellent just cooked in butter with salt and pepper and a little freshly grated nutmeg. And do not forget that spinach can also be served as a salad. Use young spinach shoots, mixed with a little vinaigrette and sprinkled with flaked almonds, fried in butter.

Salsify with crème fraîche and flat-leaf parsley

PREPARATION TIME: 25 MINUTES / COOKING TIME: 30 MINUTES

Serves 4

1 kg (2¼ lb) salsify · juice of ½ lemon
200 ml (7 fl oz) Chicken Stock (see page 66)
100 g (3½ oz) thick crème fraîche
salt and freshly ground black pepper
2 pinches of ground nutmeg
1 bunch of flat-leaf parsley

Peel the salsify and drop immediately into iced water flavoured with lemon juice. Leave them in the water for 20 minutes then drain and rinse under cold running water.

Boil the salsify in plenty of salted water for about 30 minutes.

Meanwhile, prepare the sauce: pour the Chicken Stock into a saucepan and bring to a slow boil. Add the crème fraîche, salt, pepper and nutmeg and leave to reduce by half.

Wash the flat-leaf parsley and roughly chop it then mix half of it thoroughly into the sauce.

When the salsify are tender (insert the point of a knife; if it comes out easily they are ready) drain and dry them lightly on kitchen paper to remove the excess water.

Place the rest of the chopped parsley on a large plate and roll the salsify in it to coat thoroughly. Arrange the coated salsify in a deep serving dish, pour the sauce over and serve. This vegetable is delicious with chicken, for example.

My Tip

Salsify are one of the forgotten vegetables, but if you are lucky enough to find fresh ones in the market do not hesitate to buy them as they are something you simply must try. They go wonderfully well with all white meat and poultry.

French beans with broad beans

PREPARATION TIME: 30 MINUTES / COOKING TIME: 25 MINUTES

Serves 4

**500 g (1 lb 2 oz) extra fine French beans, preferably organic or ones from Saumur
salt and freshly ground black pepper · 300 g (11 oz) fresh broad beans
50 g (2 oz) butter · 1 garlic clove · 1 bunch of chervil · 4 dried tomatoes**

Top and tail the French beans and drop them into boiling salted water or, better still, steam them. Pod the beans and steam for 15 minutes. When the vegetables are cooked, drain on kitchen paper.

Melt half the butter in a large frying pan and gently reheat the French beans and broad beans.
Peel and chop the garlic and add to the frying pan.

Mix well and cook for a further 5 minutes. When the beans are piping hot, turn off the heat, taste and adjust the seasoning then add the rest of the butter, cut into small pieces, and mix well. Chop half of the chervil and scatter over the top. Garnish with the rest of the chervil, separated into sprigs, and dried tomatoes and serve immediately with grilled meat.

Fricassee of chanterelles

PREPARATION TIME: 15 MINUTES / COOKING TIME: 15 MINUTES

Serves 4

**500 g (1 lb 2 oz) small fresh chanterelles • 30 g (1 oz) butter
salt and freshly ground black pepper • 2 garlic cloves (optional)
1 bunch of flat-leaf parsley or chervil**

Wash the chanterelles quickly under cold running water, dry them and discard the ends of the stems. Leave small ones whole but roughly chop the larger ones into pieces.

Melt the butter in a frying pan. When it begins to foam, add the chanterelles and fry them over a fairly high heat to brown them on all sides.

Season with salt and pepper. If you are using garlic, peel and chop it and fry it with the mushrooms. Wash and dry the parsley, chop half of it and add to the pan, mixing everything thoroughly together.

To serve, transfer the chanterelles to a deep serving dish, garnish with the rest of the parsley, separated into sprigs, and serve.

Flageolet beans 'au naturel'

PREPARATION TIME: 30 MINUTES / COOKING TIME: 1 HOUR 15 MINUTES

Serves 4

500 g (1lb 2 oz) small flageolet beans (white or green)
1 bouquet garni (parsley, thyme, bay leaf) • 2 onions
2 carrots • 2 garlic cloves • 1 clove • 100 g (3½ oz) butter
1 savory sprig • 1 thyme sprig • 1 rosemary sprig
salt and freshly ground black pepper
1 celery stick • 1 bunch of chervil

Wash the flageolet beans under cold running water then place them in a large saucepan and cover with water. Cover with a lid and bring to the boil over a very high heat. Turn off the heat and leave the beans to rest, covered, until they have swollen.

Drain the beans in a colander and wash under cold running water once more. Return them to the pan and cover with more cold water. Add the bouquet garni and return to the boil.

Meanwhile, peel the onions and roughly chop into large pieces. Peel the carrots and cut into round slices. Peel the garlic and leave whole. Add the vegetables, garlic and the clove to the pan then cover and leave to cook over a medium heat for about 1 hour.

Drain the flageolet beans in a colander placed over a saucepan, reserving the cooking liquor. Discard the bouquet garni. Heat half the butter in a large, cast-iron casserole and fry the onions, carrots, garlic and celery. Add the flageolet beans, sprinkle with the sprigs of savory, thyme and rosemary. Season with salt and pepper and mix well. Leave to simmer, adding a little of the reserved cooking liquor occasionally to prevent them from drying out during cooking.

When they are cooked but not yet breaking up, transfer them to a deep serving dish, dot them with the remaining butter, cut into small pieces, scatter over the chopped chervil and serve with a meat dish.

My Tip

Flageolet beans go particularly well with lamb; indeed, they are its most traditional accompaniment. They are just as good, however, served with poultry or veal.

Caramelized baby turnips

PREPARATION TIME: 20 MINUTES / COOKING TIME: 45 MINUTES

Serves 4

1.5 kg (3¼ lb) baby turnips or 1 kg (2¼ lb) long white turnips
salt and freshly ground black pepper
50 g (2 oz) butter • 5 tsp sugar

Bring a large saucepan of salted water to the boil. Meanwhile, peel the turnips, turn them into large, walnut-shaped pieces with a tablespoon. Blanch in the boiling water for 3 minutes then drain.

Melt the butter in a large, cast-iron casserole. Add the turnips and fry over a high heat for 3 minutes, turning them so that they colour evenly on all sides. Season with salt and pepper and sprinkle with the sugar. Leave to cook, uncovered, for a further 4 minutes, stirring frequently.

Reduce the heat, add a little water if necessary and leave to simmer, uncovered, for 20 minutes, stirring from time to time. The turnips should be caramelized all over.

When they are a good colour, cover the casserole and continue cooking for a further 15 minutes.

When the turnips are perfectly caramelized and still very tender, transfer them to a deep serving dish and serve with pork, beef or veal.

My Tip

The ideal accompaniment for turnips is, of course, duck. I recommend this recipe with duck 'magrets' or 'Half-wild' Duckling with Salt and Pepper (see page 142).

Ratatouille Niçoise

PREPARATION TIME: 25 MINUTES / COOKING TIME: 30 MINUTES

Serves 4

8 small white onions • 3 garlic cloves • 1 green pepper • 1 red pepper • 2 courgettes
4 tomatoes • 2 aubergines • 100 ml (3½ fl oz) olive oil • 2 thyme sprigs • 2 bay leaves
1 rosemary sprig • 3 basil leaves • 2 sage leaves • salt and freshly ground black pepper

Peel the onions and garlic and leave them whole.

Blanch the peppers in boiling water for 5 minutes, then peel, cut them in half and remove the seeds. Wash the courgettes and cut into round slices.

Blanch the tomatoes in boiling water for 1 minute then peel, cut them in half and remove the seeds.

Place all the vegetables in a large sauté pan with the olive oil, 1 thyme sprig, bay leaves, rosemary, basil and sage leaves and season with salt and pepper. Cover the pan and cook for about 20 minutes. At the end of the cooking time, uncover and continue simmering until all the water has evaporated and the vegetables are completely cooked.

Transfer the ratatouille to a large, deep serving dish, garnish with the remaining thyme sprig and serve hot with your choice of meat.

Warm vegetables in vinaigrette

PREPARATION TIME: 15 MINUTES / COOKING TIME: 15 MINUTES

Serves 4

4 purple artichokes • 1 bunch of baby carrots
8 small firm, waxy potatoes, such as Charlotte or Ratte • 1 red pepper
100 g (3½ oz) chanterelles • 8 green asparagus • 100 g (3½ oz) broad beans, podded
For the vinaigrette **4 tbsp olive oil • juice of ½ lemon • salt and freshly ground black pepper**

Wash and dry all the vegetables. Cut the artichokes in half, scrape and roughly chop the carrots and potatoes and cut the pepper into large strips. Trim the stems of the chanterelles and dry them on kitchen paper.

Cook all the vegetables in a steamer for 15 minutes.

To prepare the vinaigrette: whisk the oil and lemon juice in a bowl and season with salt and pepper.

When the vegetables are ready they should still be slightly firm. If any are still not quite cooked, steam for a few more minutes. Once cooked, transfer them all to a large salad bowl, pour over the vinaigrette and serve immediately.

Buttered potato purée

PREPARATION TIME: 30 MINUTES / COOKING TIME: 40 MINUTES

Serves 4

1 kg (2¼ lb) firm, waxy potatoes, such as Charlotte or Ratte
sea salt • 300 ml (½ pt) whole milk
250 g (9 oz) very cold butter • freshly ground black pepper

Wash the potatoes, place them, unpeeled, into a large saucepan and cover with lightly salted cold water. Cover the pan and cook over a medium heat for about 20 minutes.

When the potatoes are cooked (insert the point of a knife – if it comes out easily they are done), drain them in a large colander and set aside.

Pour the milk into a separate small saucepan and bring quickly to the boil then immediately take off the heat.

When the potatoes have cooled, peel them and pass them through the finest grid of a vegetable mill or food processor into a clean, heavy-based saucepan. Place the pan over a low heat and dry the potatoes, stirring with a wooden spoon.

Chop three-quarters of the butter into small pieces, and add slowly to the potatoes, stirring vigorously to combine until it forms a smooth purée. Next, add three-quarters of the hot milk in a thin trickle, stirring vigorously with the wooden spoon.

Pass the purée through a very fine sieve into another heavy-based saucepan, stirring it vigorously. If it seems a little dry, stir in the rest of the milk. Season with salt and pepper to taste. Stir ocssionally, add the rest of the butter and when ready to serve, reheat over a very low heat making sure it is still perfectly smooth.

My Tip

Some people prefer their potato purée creamy.
This is achieved by adding a little single cream
just before serving. Stir well as the purée
must remain smooth.

Gratin Dauphinois

PREPARATION TIME: 15 MINUTES / COOKING TIME: 1 HOUR

Serves 4

1 kg (2¼ lb) firm, waxy potatoes, such as Charlotte or Ratte
2 garlic cloves · 100 g (3½ oz) butter
salt and freshly ground black pepper · nutmeg
600 ml (1 pt) milk · 500 ml (16 fl oz) single cream
100 g (3½ oz) Comté or Emmental cheese (optional)

Peel the potatoes and slice into medium-sized rounds. Peel the garlic and cut in half.

Preheat the oven to 190°C/375°F/gas mark 5. Rub the garlic all over the inside of a large, ovenproof gratin dish. Melt the butter and together with the potatoes lay in even layers in the dish. Season with salt and pepper and grate over a little nutmeg.

Boil the milk and cream together and season with salt and pepper. Pour this over the potatoes just to cover them; be careful not to add too much liquid. Place the dish in the preheated oven and leave to cook for 45 minutes.

At the end of the cooking time remove the dish from the oven and test the potatoes with the point of a knife – the tip needs to come out easily.

When the potatoes are cooked, grate the cheese on top, if using, and return them to the oven for a further 15 minutes.

To serve, cut the gratin into 4 individual portions and serve immediately with red meat, white meat or poultry.

My Tip

Gratin Dauphinois is traditionally prepared without cheese but personally I prefer it with a crisp, golden crust on top of the potatoes, so I devised this version.

Potato pie

PREPARATION TIME: 30 MINUTES / COOKING TIME: 1 HOUR 20 MINUTES
STANDING TIME: 1 HOUR

Serves 4

For the pastry **200 g (7 oz) sifted plain flour**
150 g (5½ oz) butter • a pinch of salt
For the filling **30 g (1 oz) butter • 20 g (¾ oz) plain flour**
500 g (1 lb 2 oz) firm, waxy potatoes, such as Charlotte or Ratte
500 ml (16 fl oz) milk • 2 onions • 150 g (5½ oz) piece of smoked bacon
1 small bunch of flat-leaf parsley • 1 small bunch of basil
salt and freshly ground black pepper • 1 egg yolk
2 tbsp milk • 150 ml (¼ pt) single cream

To prepare the pastry: place the flour in a large bowl with the butter, cut into small pieces, and the salt. Mix with your fingertips, adding a little water until you have a smooth paste that can be formed into a ball. Wrap in clingfilm and leave to stand at room temperature for 1 hour.

Preheat the oven to 230°C/450°F/gas mark 8. Grease a high-sided pie dish with 10 g (¼ oz) butter. Divide the pastry into 2 unequal parts (one-third: two-thirds) and roll out on a lightly floured surface to two rounds about 2 mm (⅙ in) thick. Press the larger round into the dish, leaving the edges overhanging.

Peel the potatoes and slice finely. Bring the milk to the boil in a pan, add the potatoes and leave to cook for about 20 minutes. Peel and chop the onions and cut the bacon into lardons. Heat 20 g (¾ oz) butter in a frying pan and brown the onions and bacon lardons briefly then set aside. Roughly chop the fresh herbs.

When the potatoes are cooked, drain in a colander and mix them with the onions and bacon lardons. Season lightly with salt and pepper as the bacon is salty. Spread half of the potato mixture on the pastry and sprinkle with half of the fresh herbs. Add a second layer of potato mixture and fold the overhanging pastry in towards the centre, then cover with the smaller round of pastry and press gently to seal the edges. Beat the egg yolk with the milk and brush over the top. Then make a hole in the centre and insert a pie funnel or small rolled up piece of card to form a chimney. Bake in the preheated oven for 15 minutes then reduce the oven temperature to 200°C/400°F/gas mark 6 and cook for a further 45 minutes.

When ready to serve, lightly whisk the cream with the rest of the herbs, remove the pie from the oven and pour the cream mixture down the pie funnel or chimney, tilting the dish in every direction to distribute it evenly.

Risotto with langoustines

PREPARATION TIME: 30 MINUTES / COOKING TIME: 1 HOUR 10 MINUTES

Serves 4

**200 ml (7 fl oz) Court-bouillon (see page 42) • 1 kg (2¼ lb) langoustines
100 ml (3½ fl oz) Chicken Stock (see page 66)
100 ml (3½ fl oz) single cream • 30 g (1 oz) butter
3 shallots • 1 tbsp olive oil • 200 g (7 oz) basmati rice
salt and freshly ground black pepper • a few dried tomatoes
30 g (1 oz) Parmesan cheese shavings • 1 basil sprig
a drizzle of olive oil (optional)**

Heat the Court-bouillon in a large saucepan, add the langoustines and cook, uncovered, for 20 minutes. When they are ready, lift out with a slotted spoon and place them in a colander. Shell them, reserving any juices that escape in a large saucepan. Set the langoustines aside.

Add the Chicken Stock, cream and butter to the saucepan with the fish juices and place over a medium heat.

Peel and chop the shallots. Heat the olive oil in a sauté pan with a lid and brown the shallots. Then sprinkle in the rice and stir well until it becomes transparent. Add the Chicken Stock mixture,

season with salt and pepper, cover with a lid and leave to cook very slowly for about 30 minutes.

When the rice is soft, remove the lid, add the Parmesan cheese and mix well, then leave to cook very gently for a further 10 minutes.

When ready to serve, transfer the rice to a deep, warmed serving dish, scatter the langoustines on top and serve immediately, possibly with a few dried tomatoes, a sprinkling of Parmesan cheese shavings, a basil sprig and a final twist or two of the pepper mill. You could also drizzle a little olive oil over if you like.

My Tip

You could prepare this rice with cuttlefish or some crab claw meat instead of langoustines.

Risotto with Parmesan cheese

PREPARATION TIME: 20 MINUTES / COOKING TIME: 55 MINUTES

Serves 4

**1 bunch of onions, preferably just pulled • 1 garlic clove
100 g (3½ oz) chipolata sausages • 200 g (7 oz) button mushrooms
juice of ½ lemon • 500 ml (16 fl oz) Chicken Stock (see page 66)
100 g (3½ oz) butter • salt and freshly ground black pepper
200 g (7 oz) arborio rice • 100 g (3½ oz) Parmesan cheese**

Peel the onions and slice them into fine rings. Peel and chop the garlic. Cut the chipolata sausages into small pieces. Peel and chop the button mushrooms and moisten them immediately with lemon juice.

Heat the Chicken Stock in a large saucepan. Meanwhile, melt 40 g (1½ oz) butter in a sauté pan and sweat the onions and garlic. When they are slightly transparent, add the mushrooms and chopped sausages and let them brown. Stir well, season with salt and pepper and add the rice. When the rice is almost transparent, add just enough stock to cover it, cover with a lid and leave to cook very gently for 30 minutes, stirring often.

Keep adding more stock to make sure that the rice does not dry out. Covering the pan helps to prevent this.

When the rice is still just firm, add the remaining butter, taste and add more salt and pepper if necessary. Grate the Parmesan cheese on a fine grater and add to the rice. Stir well and leave, covered, over a very low heat for a further 3 minutes until the cheese has melted.

To serve, transfer the risotto to a large, deep serving dish and take to the table.

My Tip

This risotto with Parmesan can be made even simpler by using just onions and cheese, and makes an ideal accompaniment for a meat dish. Made according to the recipe above, it is a meal in itself.

Risotto with green asparagus tips

PREPARATION TIME: 35 MINUTES / COOKING TIME: 1 HOUR

Serves 4

2 bunches of green asparagus • 1 onion
100 ml (3½ fl oz) olive oil • 200 g (7 oz) arborio rice
1 glass of white Chardonnay • 500 ml (16 fl oz) Chicken Stock (see page 66)
salt and freshly ground black pepper • 50 g (2 oz) butter
50 g (2 oz) freshly grated Parmesan cheese
50 g (2 oz) mozzarella cheese • ½ bunch of chervil

Trim the asparagus, peel if necessary and cut into chunks. Leave the tips whole and set aside.

Peel the onion and chop finely. Pour the Chicken Stock into a large saucepan and place it over a medium heat.

Meanwhile, heat the olive oil in a sauté pan and brown the onion and asparagus stems. Add the rice and mix well.

When the rice begins to turn transparent, add the glass of wine and allow it evaporate completely while the mixture begins to soften slightly. Pour on the hot Chicken Stock, cover with a lid and cook over a very low heat, adding more liquid as often as necessary to keep the rice moist. After 20 minutes of cooking add the asparagus tips and cook until tender.

When you are ready to serve, adjust the seasoning if required, add the butter, cut into small pieces, the grated Parmesan cheese and the mozzarella cheese, cut into small pieces. Mix well and leave to stand for 10 minutes.

Transfer the risotto to a large, warmed serving dish, scatter over the chervil, finely chopped, and serve.

My Tip

You could, of course, make this into a dish suitable for a festive occasion by adding a few slices of truffle, or some morels cooked in crème fraîche.

Spaghetti with clams

PREPARATION TIME: 15 MINUTES / COOKING TIME: 30 MINUTES

Serves 4

**2 litres (3½ pints) clams • 1 glass of white wine
4 tomatoes • 5 tbsp olive oil • 1 garlic clove
1 small chilli • salt and freshly ground black pepper
½ tsp oregano • 1 tbsp flat-leaf parsley
500 g (1 lb 2 oz) spaghetti • 4 cherry tomatoes**

Brush the clams to remove any sand, rinse them well and place them in a large saucepan. Add the white wine and bring to the boil over a high heat. When the clams have opened, turn off the heat and leave to cool.

Blanch the tomatoes in boiling water for 1 minute, peel and cut them in half, remove the seeds then cut the flesh into large pieces.

Heat the olive oil in a large, cast-iron casserole. Add the garlic, peeled, and the pieces of tomato and fry for 5 minutes.

Finely chop the chilli, add to the casserole, season with salt and pepper and leave to simmer for 10 minutes. Add the oregano and parsley and mix well.

Strain the cooking liquor from the clams through a conical or fine sieve and pour it into the casserole. Take the clams out of their shells, leaving a few whole for the garnish.

Drop the spaghetti into plenty of boiling salted water and leave to cook for 7–9 minutes, depending on the thickness. When it is cooked *al dente* (still a little firm to the bite), drain and transfer it to a large, warmed serving dish. Add the clams and mix together. Garnish with the reserved whole clams and a few cherry tomatoes and serve very hot with the prepared tomato sauce.

My Tip

At the last moment you could drizzle on some extra virgin olive oil. Serve some freshly grated Parmesan cheese with this spaghetti dish.

Tagliatelle with cream and white truffles

PREPARATION TIME: 30 MINUTES / COOKING TIME: 10 MINUTES
RESTING TIME: 1 HOUR

Serves 4

For the tagliatelle **350 g (12 oz) sifted Italian pasta flour**
½ tsp salt • 3 eggs • 1 tsp olive oil
For the truffle cream **30 g (1 oz) butter • 2 garlic cloves**
100 g (3½ oz) thick crème fraîche
1 tsp cream of truffle or 1 white truffle
salt and freshly ground black pepper

To make the tagliatelle: on a large work surface, mix the flour and salt together and make a well in the centre. Break the eggs into it and begin by mixing in the flour from around the edges to form a quite rough paste then add the olive oil and knead for 15 minutes until it has become supple and shiny. Wrap the pasta dough in clingfilm and leave to rest for 1 hour.

At the end of the resting time, divide the paste into six pieces and roll them out with a rolling pin. Pass them through the rollers of a pasta cutter to turn them into tagliatelle. Your fresh pasta is now ready for use. Flour the tagliatelle lightly and leave to rest while you prepare the white truffle sauce.

To make the truffle cream sauce: melt the butter in a large frying pan and fry the peeled and crushed garlic, in a mortar. Add the crème fraîche and leave to simmer over a low heat. Add about 1 tsp of cream of truffle (if you have no cream of truffle, use a fresh white truffle, shredded on a fine grater).

Drop the prepared tagliatelle into plenty of boiling salted water and leave to cook for 1 minute, not more, so that they stay *al dente*. Drain the tagliatelle in a colander then add to the sauce in the frying pan and mix well. Transfer to a large, deep serving dish, season with salt and pepper and serve piping hot.

My Tip

The cream of truffle can be bought from Italian delis.
It is expensive, but a tube of it can last a year,
since one uses so little at a time.

Tagliatelle with queen scallops

PREPARATION TIME: 25 MINUTES / COOKING TIME: 12 MINUTES

Serves 4

**1 kg (2¼ lb) queen scallops • 2 courgettes
2 large tomatoes • 50 g (2 oz) butter, cold
generous pinch of powdered saffron
500 g (1 lb 2 oz) fresh tagliatelle (see page 176)
1 tbsp olive oil • salt and freshly ground black pepper**

Steam the queen scallops for 5 minutes to open them. Take them out of their shells, keeping a few for the garnish, and reserve the cooking juices.

Wash the courgettes and cut into thin rings. Blanch the tomatoes in boiling water then peel, cut them in half and remove the seeds. Cut the flesh into small cubes.

Prepare the saffron butter: pound the butter and saffron together, preferably in a mortar, mixing them well to combine. Mould this into a sausage shape, wrap in foil and refrigerate until required.

Cook the courgette rings for 5 minutes in a steamer (or fry them in olive oil if you prefer).

Cook the Tagliatelle and a few drops of olive oil in a large saucepan of boiling salted water for 1 minute.

When the pasta is cooked *al dente*, drain in a colander and transfer to a well-warmed large, deep serving dish. Pour over the reserved juices from the queen scallops, scatter with the courgette rings, the diced tomato, the scallops and a few round slices of the saffron butter. Mix well and season with a little salt and pepper. Garnish with the remaining whole queen scallops and serve immediately.

My Tip

Instead of queen scallops, you could use regular scallops or any other shellfish according to the season.

177

Penne with tomatoes and basil

PREPARATION TIME: 15 MINUTES / COOKING TIME: 15 MINUTES

Serves 4

500 g (1 lb 2 oz) ripe but still firm tomatoes
1 bunch of basil • 4 tbsp extra virgin olive oil
salt and freshly ground black pepper
400 g (14 oz) dried penne pasta
4 tbsp freshly grated Parmesan cheese

Blanch the tomatoes in boiling water for 1 minute.

Drain and peel, then cut them in half and remove the seeds. Cut the flesh into small cubes.

Wash the basil leaves and dry them on kitchen paper then chop finely.

Heat 3 tbsp olive oil in a saucepan. Add the tomatoes, cover with a lid and leave to stew for 5 minutes. Add half the basil, season with salt and pepper and cook for a further 5 minutes.

Bring a large saucepan of salted water to the boil and drop in the penne and cook until *al dente*, about 8 minutes. Drain the pasta and transfer to a large, warmed serving dish. Add the tomato and basil purée and mix thoroughly.

When ready to serve, sprinkle with the rest of the basil. Either mix the Parmesan cheese into the pasta or serve it separately in a small bowl, according to preference.

My Tip

I like this penne pasta quite simply boiled, but if you want to add a touch of garlic, then peel and crush it in a mortar and mix into the pasta.

Ravioli 'à la daube' with sage butter

PREPARATION TIME: 10 MINUTES / COOKING TIME: 20 MINUTES

Serves 4

1 glass of Chicken Stock (see page 66)
400 g (14 oz) best quality ready-made ravioli with filling of your choice
100 g (3½ oz) butter • 10 sage leaves • 50 g (2 oz) freshly grated Parmesan cheese
salt and freshly ground black pepper

Pour the Chicken Stock with some extra water into a saucepan and bring to the boil. Add the ravioli and cook for 10 minutes or until they rise to the surface.

While they are cooking, prepare the sage butter: melt the butter in a small saucepan. Add the sage and when the butter smells of hazelnuts and the sage has gone slightly crisp, remove the pan from the heat.

When the ravioli are cooked, drain in a colander and place them straight into a deep, warmed serving dish and pour over the sage butter you have just prepared. Sprinkle with freshly grated Parmesan cheese, season with salt and pepper and serve immediately.

DESSERTS

I am not especially fond of desserts but I adore ice cream and fruit in season, and have to confess a weakness for fruit tarts. Juicy, ripened to perfection, fruit that is not eaten fresh makes succulent preserves and jams. An apricot or rhubarb tart or crumble is truly a delight. As to strawberries and pears, they are just as good caramelized as they are cooked with wine and spices. While I am not really all that keen on sweet things, I always enjoy a good dessert.

Red berry tartlets

PREPARATION TIME: 30 MINUTES / COOKING TIME: 30 MINUTES
STANDING TIME: 1 HOUR

Serves 4

**15 g (½ oz) butter · plain flour · 80 ml (3¼ fl oz) milk
1 punnet wild strawberries · 1 punnet 'mara' (cultivated version of 'wild') strawberries
1 punnet raspberries · 1 punnet bilberries (optional) · icing sugar
For the shortbread pastry ½ tsp baking powder · a pinch of salt
150 g (5 oz) plain flour · 1 tbsp caster sugar · 75 g (3 oz) softened butter · 1 egg yolk
For the confectioner's custard 400 ml (14 fl oz) milk · 2 vanilla pods
30 g (1 oz) cornflour · 80 g (3¼ oz) caster sugar · 5 egg yolks · 30 g (1 oz) butter
For the 'mousseline' cream 2 tbsp kirsch · 20 g (¾ oz) unsalted butter**

To prepare the shortbread pastry: mix the baking powder, salt and flour together in a bowl then pile it on a pastry board and make a well in the centre. Place the sugar, the well-softened butter, cut into small pieces, and the egg yolk into the well and work it until it forms a light, sandy-textured paste. Add a little water and mix until a soft dough forms, then roll it into a ball, wrap in clingfilm and leave to rest for at least 1 hour, if possible longer.

To prepare the confectioner's custard: heat the milk in a saucepan with the vanilla pods, split in half lenghways, the cornflour and half the sugar. Beat the egg yolks with the remaining sugar until they turn white then dilute with a little of the hot milk mixture and mix well. Pour the egg mixture into the saucepan with the rest of the milk. Whisk thoroughly and place over a medium heat. When the mixture has thickened, turn off the heat and leave to cool.

Remove the vanilla pods, scrape out the seeds and add the seeds back to the mixture. Beat the butter, a little at a time, into the custard to make it richer then set the pan on a bed of crushed ice to cool rapidly.

Preheat the oven to 240°C/475°F/gas mark 9. Grease 4 large tartlet tins with the 15 g (½ oz) butter. Unwrap the pastry and roll it out on a lightly floured board 1 cm (½ in) thick, taking care not to break it, as it is very delicate. Cut 4 discs, 12 cm (4½ in) in diameter, and use to line the greased tins. Bake in the preheated hot oven for 5 minutes then leave to cool completely.

Prepare the 'mousseline' cream by whisking the confectioner's custard together with the kirsch and butter to a smooth, creamy consistency. Spread a layer into each of the cooled tartlets, pile in the fruit, dust with icing sugar and serve immediately.

Raspberry clafoutis with pistachio nuts

PREPARATION TIME: 45 MINUTES / COOKING TIME: 20 MINUTES
RESTING TIME: 1 HOUR

Serves 4

15 g (½ oz) butter · **plain flour** · **500 g (1lb 2 oz) fresh raspberries**
50 g (2 oz) shelled pistachio nuts
For the clafoutis mixture **200 ml (7 fl oz) single cream**
25 g (1 oz) plain flour · **75 g (3 oz) sugar** · **2 eggs, separated**
For the shortbread pastry **½ tsp baking powder** · **a pinch of salt**
150 g (5 oz) plain flour · **1 tbsp sugar**
75 g (3 oz) softened butter · **1 egg yolk**

To prepare the shortbread pastry: mix the baking powder, salt and flour together in a bowl then pile it on a pastry board and make a well in the centre. Place the sugar, the well-softened butter, cut into small pieces, and the egg yolk into the well and work it together until it forms a light, sandy-textured paste. Add a little water and mix until a soft dough forms. Roll it into a ball, wrap in clingfilm and leave to rest for at least 1 hour.

To prepare the clafoutis mixture: whisk the cream, together with the flour, sugar and the 2 egg yolks in a large bowl.

Preheat the oven to 200°C/400°F/gas mark 6. Grease a large tart tin with a little butter.

Roll out the pastry thinly on a lightly floured board. Carefully line the tin with it and bake blind (lined with greaseproof paper weighted with dried beans) in the oven for 10 minutes. Leave to cool then arrange the raspberries over the base of the pastry case and pour the clafoutis mixture over the top. Bake in the oven for a further 10 minutes.

Remove the clafoutis from the oven and leave to stand until it is just warm. Alternatively, leave until it is completely cold, then sprinkle it with the roughly chopped pistachio nuts and serve.

My Tip

You can use different fruit for this recipe: cherries, apricots, peaches or plums. Use what is in season, or choose your favourite.

Apricot crumble with almonds

PREPARATION TIME: 35 MINUTES / COOKING TIME: 35 MINUTES

Serves 4

For the crumble **100 g (3½ oz) sifted flour** · **100 g (3½ oz) sugar**
about 7 g (⅙ oz) vanilla sugar · **100 g (3½ oz) unsalted butter**
For the filling **50 g (2 oz) butter** · **1 kg (2¼ lb) apricots, preferably**
organic or ones from the Roussillon province · **about 7 g (⅙ oz) vanilla sugar**
100 g (3½ oz) flaked almonds

Mix the flour, sugar and vanilla sugar together in a large bowl. Add the butter, cut into small pieces, and rub into the flour with your fingertips until the mixture resembles breadcrumbs.

Wash the apricots, halve them and take out the stones then place the fruit in a saucepan. Add the vanilla sugar and cook until they are lightly caramelized.

Preheat the oven to 230°C/450°F/gas mark 8. Grease a large tart tin with a little butter.

Arrange the apricots, cut side down, in the base of the tin, cover with the crumble mixture and bake in the hot oven for about 30 minutes.

When the crumble is cooked, remove from the oven and leave until it is just warm. Alternatively, leave to cool completely.

Melt the 50 g (2 oz) butter in a large frying pan and fry the flaked almonds briefly then drain on kitchen paper. Scatter over the crumble and serve immediately.

My Tip

This crumble is equally good hot, warm or cold.
You can either transfer it to a serving dish,
or take it directly to the table and serve
straight from the tin.

Meringue with red berries

PREPARATION TIME: 30 MINUTES / COOKING TIME: 20 MINUTES

Serves 4

For the meringues **125 g (4 oz) egg white • 250 g (9 oz) caster sugar
2 drops vanilla extract • 15 g (½ oz) butter • a little plain flour**
For the decoration **100 ml (3½ fl oz) whipping cream • 1 heaped tbsp icing sugar
500 ml (16 fl oz) raspberry or strawberry sorbet • 1 punnet raspberries
1 punnet wild strawberries or 'mara' (cultivated version of 'wild') strawberries**

To prepare the meringues: Whisk the egg white until quite firm then add 1 tbsp sugar and the vanilla extract and continue whisking, adding the rest of the sugar gradually.

Preheat the oven to 120°C/250°F/gas mark ½. Using a piping bag, form the mixture into 8 cm (3¼ in) discs on a greased and lightly floured baking sheet, flatten them and cook for 2 hours with the oven door slightly ajar. Leave to cool.

Whip the cream to a light, soft texture and fold in the icing sugar. Cover one disc of meringue with sorbet, set another meringue disc on top and coat with a layer of whipped cream then decorate with the fruit you have selected.

Vanilla slice

PREPARATION TIME: 30 MINUTES / COOKING TIME: 20 MINUTES

Serves 4

For the Confectioner's Custard **See page 182**
For the puff pastry **6 discs prepared puff pastry**
To decorate **3 tbsp icing sugar**

Prepare the Confectioner's Custard according to the recipe on page 182.

To make the puff pastry slices: bake 6 discs or rectangles of prepared puff pastry for about 20 minutes. When the edges are cooked, take them out and leave to cool completely.

To assemble the vanilla slices: spread a layer of custard on the first pastry disc or rectangle with a spatula and place a second one on top. Continue until all the pastry is used then sift the icing sugar on the top. Set aside until required.

Caramelized fondant cake made with three types of apple

PREPARATION TIME: 30 MINUTES / COOKING TIME: 1 HOUR 15 MINUTES

Serves 4

1 kg (2¼ lb) Belle de Boskoop apples • 1 kg (2¼ lb) russet apples
1 kg (2¼ lb) Pink Lady apples • 2 tbsp water • 100 g (3½ oz) sugar
100 g (3½ oz) butter • 4 large eggs
For the caramel **200 g (7 oz) sugar • 100 ml (3½ fl oz) water**

To prepare the caramel: place the sugar and water in a large saucepan and boil over a low heat until it turns a light amber in colour. Leave to cool.

Pour the caramel into a deep cake tin, tilting it so that it coats the whole of the base, then leave to harden slightly.

Peel the apples, cut them into quarters and remove the cores. Slice them finely. Place them in a large saucepan with the water and cook for about 5 minutes. When the apples are reduced to a purée, stir in the sugar and leave to cook for a further 15 minutes, adding a little more water if necessary. Leave to cool.

Cut the butter into small pieces and add to the apple mixture then break in the eggs, one by one. Mix thoroughly to a smooth consistency then pour into the prepared caramel-lined cake tin.

Preheat the oven to 160°C/325°F/gas mark 3. Prepare a bain-marie by part-filling a large roasting tin with boiling water, then set the cake tin with the apples in it and bake in the hot oven for about 1 hour.

When it is cooked, at which time the crust will be slightly browned on the surface, remove the cake from the oven and leave in a cool place. Serve warm or completely cold, whichever you prefer.

My Tip

I like to serve this apple fondant just as it is, but just occasionally I coat it with a thin layer of meringue (see page 186) and grill until light golden in colour.

Rhubarb tart

PREPARATION TIME: 1 HOUR / COOKING TIME: 55 MINUTES
RESTING TIME: 3 HOURS

Serves 4

1 kg (2¼ lb) rhubarb · **about 50 g (2 oz) granulated sugar**
15 g (½ oz) butter · **a little plain flour** · **3 whole eggs**
250 g (9 oz) soft brown sugar · **100 ml (3½ fl oz) single cream**
50 g (2 oz) hazelnuts
For the shortcrust pastry **100 g (3½ oz) butter** · **200 g (7 oz) plain flour**
a pinch of salt · **1 tbsp sugar** · **3 tbsp water**

To prepare the shortcrust pastry: cut the butter into small pieces and mix with the flour, salt and sugar then work with the fingertips until it resembles breadcrumbs. Add a little water and mix to a supple but not sticky dough then knead lightly and form the dough into a ball. Wrap in clingfilm and leave to rest for 3 hours if possible.

Wash the sticks of rhubarb and trim the ends then cut into short lengths and cook in sweetened water for 10 minutes.

Preheat the oven to 180°C/350°F/gas mark 4. Grease a large, ovenproof pie dish or pie plate with butter.

Roll out the pastry on a floured work surface and use to line the greased pie dish. Cover the base with the rhubarb pieces, packed tightly together.

To prepare the cream: beat the eggs and soft brown sugar together. Stir in the cream and pour this mixture over the rhubarb. Bake in the hot oven for about 45 minutes.

After 40 minutes, remove the tart from the oven and scatter the hazelnuts, roughly chopped, over the top, then return the tart to the oven for a further 5 minutes.

Remove the tart from the oven and leave until just warm or until cold.

My Tip

Soft brown sugar is unrefined and very dark in colour.
It is extensively used in the north of France.
In this recipe it gives a quite distinctive
flavour to the rhubarb.

Pear tart with almonds

PREPARATION TIME: 25 MINUTES / COOKING TIME: 30–40 MINUTES

Serves 4

**15 g (½ oz) butter • 350 g (12 oz) Shortcrust Pastry (see page 189) • a little plain flour
4 pears • 50 g (2 oz) sugar • about 7 g (⅙ oz) vanilla sugar
For the cream 200 ml (7 fl oz) milk • 2 whole eggs • 30 g (1 oz) sugar • 15 g (½ oz) cornflour
30 g (1 oz) ground almonds • 40 g (1½ oz) crème fraîche**

Preheat the oven to 200°C/400°F/gas mark 6. Grease a large pie dish with the butter. Roll out the pastry on a lightly floured surface and use to line the dish.

Peel the pears, cut in half and remove the cores. Place them in a large saucepan, cover with water, add the sugar and vanilla sugar and boil for 10 minutes.

To prepare the cream: heat the milk in a saucepan.

Whisk the eggs and sugar together in a large bowl until the mixture turns white. Stir in the cornflour then pour on the hot milk, stirring constantly with a wooden spoon. Return the mixture to the saucepan and continue heating until thickened. Add the almonds and crème fraîche, mix well and leave to cool. Pour the cooled cream into the pastry case and arrange the pears on the top. Bake in the hot oven for about 30–40 minutes, then serve.

Chocolate tart

PREPARATION TIME: 30 MINUTES / COOKING TIME: 20–30 MINUTES

Serves 4

**Shortbread pastry (see page 184) • 80 ml (5½ tbsp) milk • 200 ml (7 fl oz) single cream
200 g (7 oz) plain dark chocolate, at least 53 per cent cocoa solids • 2 eggs • 15 g (½ oz) butter
a little plain flour • icing sugar**

Make the shortbread pastry as in page 184.

Prepare the chocolate mixture by heating the milk and cream in a large saucepan. Roughly chop the chocolate and place in a heatproof bowl. Break the eggs into the bowl and add the hot milk and cream, stirring vigorously.

Preheat the oven to 200°C/400°F/gas mark 6. Grease a large tart tin with the butter. Roll out the pastry on a lightly floured surface and use to line the greased tin then bake blind (lined with grease-proof paper weighted with dried beans) for 15–20 minutes. When the pastry is lightly browned, remove from the oven and leave to cool.

Pour the chocolate mixture into the pastry case and bake for 5–10 minutes. Remove – the centre should still be slightly wobbly – and cool completely. Dust with icing sugar and serve well chilled.

Cream cheese tart with wild strawberries

PREPARATION TIME: 45 MINUTES / COOKING TIME: 20 MINUTES
RESTING TIME: 24 HOURS IF POSSIBLE / PREPARE THE DAY BEFORE

Serves 4

**plain flour • 15 g (½ oz) butter • 200 g (7 oz) whipping cream
600 g (1¼ lb) smooth cream cheese • 500 g (1 lb 2 oz) wild strawberries
sifted icing sugar**
For the shortbread pastry **½ tsp baking powder • a pinch of salt
150 g (5 oz) plain flour • 1 tbsp caster sugar
75 g (3 oz) softened butter • 1 egg yolk**

To make the shortbread pastry: mix the baking powder, salt and flour together then heap it on a pastry board and make a well in the centre. Place the sugar, the well-softened butter, cut into small pieces, and the egg yolk into the well and work it until it forms a light, sandy-textured paste. Add a little water and mix until a smooth dough forms. Roll into a ball, wrap in clingfilm and leave to rest for 24 hours if possible.

Roll out the pastry on a lightly floured board, taking care not to break it, as it is very delicate.

Preheat the oven to 240°C/475°F/gas mark 9. Grease a large tart tin with the butter.

Line the tin with the pastry and bake in the hot oven for about 20 minutes. When the pastry case is cooked, leave to cool.

Whip the cream until very stiff. Whisk the cream cheese vigorously then fold it into the whipped cream. If it is not to be used immediately, store in the refrigerator.

To assemble the tart, spread the prepared cream in the pastry case, pile on the wild strawberries in a pyramid, dust with a little sifted icing sugar and take to the table.

My Tip

This cream cheese tart can be prepared in several stages, which is an advantage. The pastry case is pre-cooked and can be used any time within two or three days if kept in a cool place wrapped in clingfilm.

Rum baba with crystallized pineapple

PREPARATION TIME: 30 MINUTES / COOKING TIME: 40 MINUTES
RISING TIME: 1 HOUR

Serves 4

100 g (3½ oz) raisins • **200 ml (7 fl oz) aged rum**
20 g (¾ oz) fresh yeast • **2 tbsp warm water**
200 g (7 oz) sifted plain flour • **30 g (1 oz) caster sugar**
salt • **4 eggs** • **100 g (3½ oz) softened butter**
For the syrup **100 ml (3½ fl oz) water** • **500 g (1 lb 2 oz) sugar**
zest of 1 lemon • **zest of 1 orange** • **1 vanilla pod**
200 ml (7 fl oz) aged rum
For the caramelized pineapple **1 pineapple, preferably organic**
or one from Pretoria • **30 g (1 oz) sugar cane syrup**

Place the raisins in a bowl, pour over the rum and leave to soak. Meanwhile, dissolve the yeast in the warm water. Pile the flour in a heap on a large work surface, preferably marble, and make a well in the centre. Place the sugar, salt, 2 eggs and the dissolved yeast into the well and stir with a wooden spoon until it forms an elastic dough. Add another egg and mix well, then add the last egg and 80 g (3¼ oz) softened butter. When all the ingredients are kneaded together into a very elastic dough, add the raisins, drained, and knead again to incorporate them. Leave the dough to rise for 1 hour at room temperature, covered with a clean cloth.

Grease 16 small baba moulds or a large savarin mould with the remaining butter.

Preheat the oven to 240°C/475°F/gas mark 9. When the dough has doubled in size, divide it between the 16 small moulds or place it in the large one and bake in the hot oven for 12 minutes, in the case of the small ones, or 30 minutes for the large one.

When the babas are cooked, turn them out of the moulds and leave to cool.

To prepare the syrup: boil the water and sugar together to make a thick syrup (or use ready-made sugar cane syrup). Stir in the lemon and orange zest, vanilla pod and rum then soak the babas in the hot syrup until bubbles no longer rise to the surface. Remove and leave to drain on a wire rack.

Meanwhile, prepare the caramelized pineapple: peel the pineapple and cut into quarters. Remove the hard central core and cut the flesh into small cubes. Place them in the sugar cane syrup over a low heat and leave until they become saturated with the syrup. When the pineapple cubes are well coated, leave them to caramelize.

Serve the babas on individual plates, surrounded by cubes of the caramelized pineapple.

If you have used a savarin mould, fill the centre with the caramelized pineapple cubes.

Warm cherries with pistachio nuts

PREPARATION TIME: 40 MINUTES / COOKING TIME: 30 MINUTES

Serves 4

1 kg (2¼ lb) black cherries, preferably organic or ones from the Roussillon province
50 g (2 oz) caster sugar • 1 vanilla pod • 200 g (7 oz) pistachio nuts • 50 g (2 oz) butter

Wash and drain the cherries then dry on kitchen paper. Remove the stalks and place the cherries in a large sauté pan. Cover with water, add the sugar, split the vanilla pod in half, scrape out the seeds and add them to the cherries. Leave to simmer over a very low heat for about 20 minutes.

While the cherries are cooking, chop the pistachio nuts and set aside.

When the cherry 'soup' is ready, lift out the cherries and place them in a deep serving dish and leave until just warm.

Reduce the cooking liquor over a medium heat until it forms a fairly thick syrup. Pour this syrup over the fruit and sprinkle with the chopped pistachio nuts. Serve this cherry 'soup' either warm or cold. Vanilla ice cream goes well with this dish.

Apricots with almond milk

PREPARATION TIME: 15 MINUTES / COOKING TIME: 20 MINUTES
INFUSING TIME: 1 HOUR

Serves 4

**200 ml (7 fl oz) milk • 100 g (3½ oz) ground almonds • 50 g (2 oz) caster sugar
1 kg (2¼ lb) ripe apricots, preferably organic or ones from the Roussillon province • 1 tsp cornflour**

To prepare the almond milk: warm the milk, ground almonds and sugar together, then leave for 1 hour to infuse. Strain the milk through a conical or fine sieve, pressing it well to extract all the flavour and pour into a clean saucepan.

Bring a large saucepan of water to the boil. Add the apricots and cook for about 10 minutes, then drain in a colander and rinse under cold running water.

Peel the skins, cut in half and remove the stones.

Reheat the almond milk gently. Stir in the cornflour and cook until it thickens then leave to cool.

Arrange the half apricots in a serving dish, pour over the almond milk until the apricots are coated and take them to the table, possibly accompanied with some strawberries or raspberries.

Strawberries in Anjou wine

PREPARATION TIME: 30 MINUTES / NO COOKING REQUIRED
MARINATING TIME: 24 HOURS / PREPARE THE DAY BEFORE

Serves 4

1 kg (2¼ lb) strawberries, preferably 'mara' or 'gariguettes'
(cultivated varieties of small, 'wild' strawberry)
100 g (3½ oz) sugar
100 ml (3½ fl oz) French red wine, preferably Anjou

The day before you need them, hull the strawberries and place them in a bowl with the sugar. Pour over the wine and leave to marinate for 24 hours.

The next day, pour half of the strawberries and half of the marinade into a blender and process until smooth. Set aside the rest of the marinade. Churn the mixture in an ice-cream machine then transfer to the freezer to set.

When the strawberry sorbet is set and you are ready to serve, place the rest of the strawberries, cut in half, on dessert plates or in long-stemmed wine glasses, add a ball of the sorbet and pour over the rest of the marinade.

My Tip

My chef, Laurent Audiot, used to prepare these strawberries with Bandol, a delicately flavoured wine from Provence. I recommend that you, too, try this recipe made with Bandol.

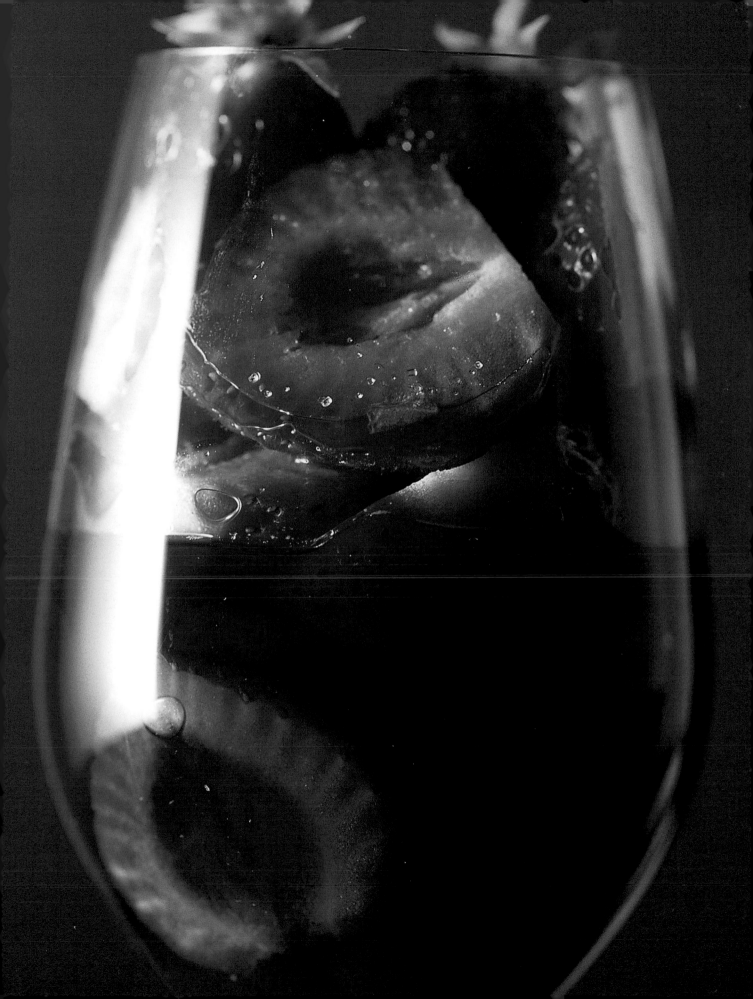

Pear soup with wine and spices

PREPARATION TIME: 30 MINUTES / COOKING TIME: 15 MINUTES

Serves 4

6 ripe but still firm pears
500 ml (16 fl oz) vanilla ice cream
For the syrup **4 sugar cubes**
1 bottle French red wine, preferably Bourgueil
½ tsp ground cinnamon
2 star anise · 1 vanilla pod

Prepare the syrup in which to cook the pears: mix the sugar and red wine together in a saucepan. Add the cinnamon and star anise. Split the vanilla pod lengthwise and scrape out the seeds from the interior then stir everything together and bring to the boil over a medium heat.

Peel the pears and cut them into quarters. Remove the cores and poach in the prepared syrup.

After 8 minutes they will be cooked. Turn off the heat and leave to soak in the syrup for 30 minutes.

To serve, lift out the pears and arrange them on dessert plates. Reduce the syrup over a high heat and leave to cool, then pour over the pears and serve immediately with a scoop of vanilla ice cream.

My Tip

This fruit soup can also be prepared with 'pêches de vigne' – a variety of peach grown in the Lyons region – or with yellow or sweet purple plums. It is important to use fruit that is very juicy.

Curd cheese with red berries

PREPARATION TIME: 15 MINUTES / NO COOKING REQUIRED
CHILLING TIME: 1 HOUR

Serves 4

4 small curd cheeses
100 ml (3½ fl oz) whipping cream
2 tbsp icing sugar
100 g (3½ oz) wild strawberries
100 g (3½ oz) raspberries
100 g (3½ oz) bilberries
4 mint leaves
almond 'tuiles' (see my tip, optional)

Drain the curd cheeses on a wire rack for about 15 minutes.

Place the whipping cream in a large bowl, whip to form soft peaks, then add 1 tbsp icing sugar.

Wash the fruit and dry on kitchen paper then place half of them in a blender or food processor and process to a coulis. Strain through a fine sieve.

Set the well-drained curd cheese on dessert plates, surround with the remaining fruit and decorate by piping the whipped cream on top. Dredge with the rest of the icing sugar, top with a mint leaf and leave in the refrigerator for at least 1 hour.

Before serving, pour over the coulis and take to the table, perhaps accompanied with some almond 'tuiles' or wafers.

My Tip

You could equally well coat the curd cheeses with runny acacia or lavender honey. 'Tuiles' are thin, crisp tile-shaped biscuits.

Crème caramel

PREPARATION TIME: 20 MINUTES / COOKING TIME: 30 MINUTES
COOLING TIME: 30 MINUTES

Serves 4

15 g (½ oz) butter
500 ml (16 fl oz) milk
2 vanilla pods
4 eggs plus 1 egg yolk
50 g (2 oz) sugar
For the caramel **2 tbsp water**
10 sugar cubes

Preheat the oven to 200°C/400°F/gas mark 6. Grease 4 ramekins with the butter.

To prepare the caramel: boil the water with the sugar cubes in a saucepan until it forms a pale golden caramel. Divide the caramel between the ramekins, tilting them in all directions to coat the base and sides. Leave to cool completely.

Heat the milk gently with the vanilla pods, split in half, in a large saucepan. After simmering for 5 minutes remove the vanilla pods, scrape out the seeds and add them to the milk.

Beat the whole eggs, the extra yolk and the sugar in a large bowl until white and frothy, then pour in the milk in a thin stream, stirring constantly with a wooden spoon. When the mixture is combined, strain through a conical or fine sieve and pour it into the ramekins.

Prepare a bain-marie by filling a deep roasting tin two-thirds full with boiling water and setting the ramekins in it. Bake in the hot oven for about 20 minutes.

Remove the ramekins from the oven while the crème caramels are still slightly wobbly in the centre and leave them until just warm or completely cold. You could serve them in the ramekins or turn them out onto individual serving plates.

My Tip

If you wish to flavour these crème caramels with orange or lemon zest, blanch it before adding it to the milk.

INDEX

A

Apricot crumble with almonds 185
Apricots with almond milk 197
Artichokes 'barigoule' 157
Asparagus with mustard sauce 155

B

Baby squid sautéed Luzienne
    style 103
Baby squid with garlic and
    parsley 103
Back steaks of fresh cod 95
Beef bourguignon 132
Beef carpaccio 127
Beef in white wine 133
Blanquette of veal cooked
    the old-fashioned way 118
Bouillabaisse 76
Brandade of salt cod 96
Breton lobster salad 40
Broad bean soup 69
Buttered potato purée 166

C

Calf's head with gribiche sauce 122
Calf's liver Lyonnaise style 123
Capon 'cooked in the pot' 79
Caramelized chicory 152
Caramelized fondant cake made
    with three types of apple 188
Caramelized baby turnips 163
Carpaccio of fresh tuna with basil 34
Cassoulet 78
Chocolate tart 191
Cream cheese tart with wild
    strawberries 192
Cream of artichokes with
    chestnuts 67
Cream of green asparagus with
    sorrel 66
Cream of lentil soup with
    langoustines and rosemary 73
Crème caramel 202
Curd cheese with red berries 201
Curly endive with bacon lardons 53

D

Duck with turnips 146

E

Eggs 'meurette' 56
Entrecôte bordelaise 128

F

Farmer's soup 71
Flageolet beans 'au naturel' 162
Flank of sirloin with shallots 129
Foie gras in Muscat wine 54
French beans with broad beans 160
Fresh tuna with chanterelles 0
Freshwater crayfish 'à la nage' 112
Fried baby squid 104
Fricassee of chicken with
    crayfish 147
Fricassee of chanterelles 161

G

Gratin Dauphinois 168
Green asparagus with vierge
    sauce 156
Grenadins of veal with broad beans
    and chanterelles 124
Grilled langoustines 108
Guinea fowl with cabbage 148

H

'Half-wild' duckling with salt and
    pepper 142
Ham with parsley,
    Burgundy style 44

J

Jellied rabbit 46

L

Lamb curry 141
Leeks with vinaigrette 52
Lobster à l'armoricaine 110
Lobsters 'à la nage' 109

M

Mackerel in white wine 38
Mackerel rillettes 35
Marinated fresh anchovies with
    potatoes 32
Meltingly soft crab 42
Meringue with red berries 186
Minestrone 64
Monkfish à l'américaine 102
Moules marinière 106
Mussel soup with saffron 74

N

Navarin of milk-fed spring lamb
    with basil 84

O

Ox cheek with carrots and
  calf's feet 134
Ox muzzle with vinaigrette 49

P

Pâté Lorraine 45
Pear soup with wine and spices 200
Pear tart with almonds 190
Penne with tomatoes and basil 178
Peppers marinated in olive oil 52
Petits pois French style 154
Pesto soup 72
Pigeon pot-au-feu 81
Pink bream tartare 39
Pink garlic soup 68
Pork brawn 48
Pork chops charcutière style 139
Pork fillet with mustard sauce 135
Pork loin stuffed with herbs 136
Potato pie 169
Pot-au-feu with four types
  of meat 87
Pressed oxtail with leeks 50

Q

Quiche Lorraine 58

R

Rabbit with rosemary 149
Raspberry clafoutis with pistachio
  nuts 184
Ratatouille Niçoise 164
Ravioli 'à la daube' with
  sage butter 179

Ravioli filled with langoustines and
  flat-leaf parsley 60
Red berry tartlets 182
Red mullet with saffron 101
Rhubarb tart 189
Risotto with green asparagus
  tips 173
Risotto with langoustines 170
Risotto with Parmesan cheese 172
Roast knuckle of milk-fed veal
  with vinegar 120
Rum baba with crystallized
  pineapple 194

S

Salmon with warm potatoes 36
Salsify with crème fraîche and
  flat-leaf parsley 159
Salt cod with aïoli sauce 94
Salt pork with lentils 83
Sardines marinated in olive oil 98
Sauerkraut 82
Scallops with artichokes 113
Scrambled eggs with asparagus
  tips 57
Skate wings with capers and
  lemon 97
Slow-cooked milk-fed lamb
  with spices and dried fruit 140
Small chicken cooked in vin jaune
  with morels 145
Small chicken with Diable
  sauce 144
Small stuffed Provençal-style
  vegetables 86

Smoked haddock with 'boulangère'
  potatoes 93
Snails in parsley butter 61
Soles meunière 100
Spaghetti with clams 174
Spare ribs with honey and spices 138
Spinach with double cream 158
Steak tartare made with tail-end of
  fillet 126
Strawberries in Anjou wine 198
Strung fillet of beef 130
Stuffed squid 105

T

Tagliatelle with cream and white
  truffles 176
Tagliatelle with queen scallops 177
Terrine Lorraine 45
Tomato and pumpkin soup 70
Tuna steak with artichokes,
  flavoured with curry 92

V

Vanilla slice 187
Veal cutlets with tarragon 119
Veal flank with caramelized carrots
  and small onions 116

W

Warm cherries with pistachio
  nuts 196
Warm vegetables in vinaigrette 165
Whiting Colbert 99
Wild rabbit stew with
  fresh pasta 80

INDEX OF RECIPES

ENTRÉES

Breton lobster salad 40
Carpaccio of fresh tuna
    with basil 34
Curly endive with bacon lardons 53
Eggs 'meurette' 56
Foie gras in Muscat wine 54
Ham with parsley,
    Burgundy style 44
Jellied rabbit 46
Leeks with vinaigrette 52
Mackerel in white wine 38
Mackerel rillettes 35
Marinated fresh anchovies
    with potatoes 32
Meltingly soft crab 42
Ox muzzle with vinaigrette 49
Peppers marinated in olive oil 52
Pink bream tartare 39
Pork brawn 48
Pressed oxtail with leeks 50
Quiche Lorraine 58
Ravioli filled with langoustines and
    flat-leaf parsley 60
Salmon with warm potatoes 36
Scrambled eggs with asparagus
    tips 57
Snails in parsley butter 61
Terrine Lorraine 45

SOUPS AND ONE-POT MEALS

Bouillabaisse 76
Broad bean soup 69
Capon 'cooked in the pot' 79
Cassoulet 78
Cream of artichokes with
    chestnuts 67
Cream of green asparagus with
    sorrel 66
Cream of lentil soup with
    langoustines and rosemary 73
Farmer's soup 71
Minestrone 64
Mussel soup with saffron 74
Navarin of milk-fed spring lamb
    with basil 84
Pesto soup 72
Pigeon pot-au-feu 81
Pink garlic soup 68
Pot-au-feu with four types
    of meat 87
Salt pork with lentils 83
Sauerkraut 82
Small stuffed Provençal-style
    vegetables 86
Tomato and pumpkin soup 70
Wild rabbit stew with
    fresh pasta 80

FISH AND SHELLFISH

Baby squid sautéed Luzienne
    style 103
Baby squid with garlic and
    parsley 103
Back steaks of fresh cod 95
Brandade of salt cod 96
Fresh tuna with chanterelles 90
Freshwater crayfish 'à la nage' 112
Fried baby squid 104
Grilled langoustines 108
Lobster à l'armoricaine 110
Lobsters 'à la nage' 109
Monkfish à l'américaine 102
Moules marinière 106
Red mullet with saffron 101
Salt cod with aïoli sauce 94
Sardines marinated in olive oil 98
Scallops with artichokes 113
Skate wings with capers and
    lemon 97
Smoked haddock with 'boulangère'
    potatoes 93
Soles meunière 100
Stuffed squid 105
Tuna steak with artichokes,
    flavoured with curry 92
Whiting Colbert 99

MEAT AND POULTRY

Beef bourguignon 132
Beef carpaccio 127
Beef in white wine 133
Blanquette of veal cooked in the
    old way 118
Calf's head with gribiche sauce 122
Calf's liver Lyonnaise style 123
Duck with turnips 146
Entrecôte bordelaise 128
Flank of sirloin with shallots 129
Fricassee of chicken with
    crayfish 147
Grenadins of veal with broad beans
    and chanterelles 124
Guinea fowl with cabbage 148

'Half-wild' duckling with salt and
    pepper 142
Lamb curry 141
Ox cheek with carrots and calf's
    feet 134
Pork chops charcutière style 139
Pork fillet with mustard sauce 135
Pork loin stuffed with herbs 136
Rabbit with rosemary 149
Roast knuckle of milk-fed veal
    with vinegar 120
Slow-cooked milk-fed lamb with
    spices and dried fruit 140
Small chicken cooked in vin jaune
    with morels 145
Small chicken with Diable
    sauce 144
Spare ribs with honey and
    spices 138
Steak tartare made with tail-end
    of fillet 126
Strung fillet of beef 130
Veal cutlets with tarragon 119
Veal flank with caramelized carrots
    and small onions 116

VEGETABLES AND SIDE DISHES

Artichokes 'barigoule' 157
Asparagus with mustard sauce 155
Braised chicory 152
Buttered potato purée 166
Caramelized chicory 152
Caramelized baby turnips 163
Flageolet beans 'au naturel' 162

French beans with broad beans 160
Fricassee of chanterelles 161
Gratin Dauphinois 168
Green asparagus with vierge
    sauce 156
Penne with tomatoes and basil 178
Petits pois French style 154
Potato pie 169
Ratatouille Niçoise 164
Ravioli 'à la daube' with sage
    butter 179
Risotto with green asparagus
    tips 173
Risotto with langoustines 170
Risotto with Parmesan cheese 172
Salsify with crème fraîche and
    flat-leaf parsley 159
Spaghetti with clams 174
Spinach with double cream 158
Tagliatelle with cream and white
    truffles 176
Tagliatelle with queen scallops 177
Warm vegetables in vinaigrette 165

DESSERTS

Apricot crumble with almonds 185
Apricots with almond milk 197
Caramelized fondant cake made
    with three types of apple 188
Chocolate tart 191
Cream cheese tart with wild
    strawberries 192
Crème caramel 202
Curd cheese with red berries 201
Meringue with red berries 186

Pear soup with wine and spices 200
Pear tart with almonds 190
Raspberry clafoutis with pistachio
    nuts 184
Red berry tartlets 182
Rhubarb tart 189
Rum baba with crystallized
    pineapple 194
Strawberries in Anjou wine 198
Vanilla slice 187
Warm cherries with pistachio
    nuts 196